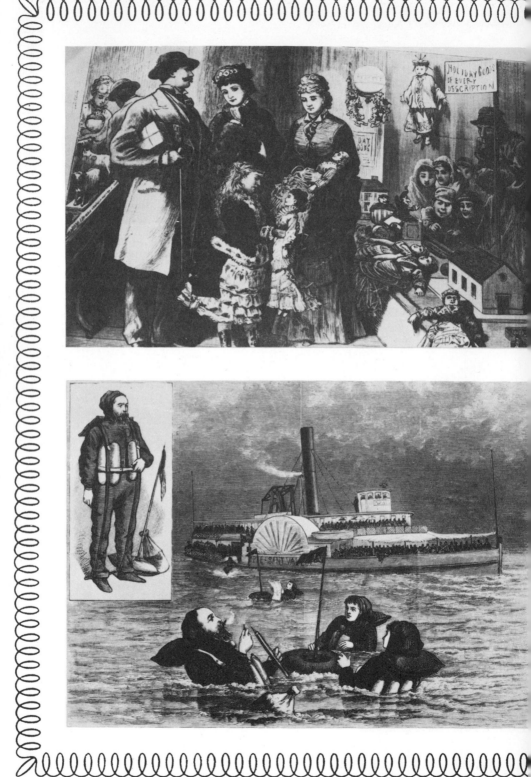

THE WAY IT WAS—1876

WESTMINSTER PRESS BOOKS

BY SUZANNE HILTON

The Way It Was—1876

Beat It, Burn It, and Drown It

It's a Model World

It's Smart to Use a Dummy

How Do They Cope With It?

How Do They Get Rid of It?

THE WAY IT WAS—
1876

---

by *Suzanne Hilton*

THE WESTMINSTER PRESS
PHILADELPHIA

Published by the Westminster Press®
Philadelphia, Pennsylvania
Second printing, 1975
Printed in the United States of America

PICTURE CREDITS: Bell Telephone Company of Pa., p. 174; Butterick Patterns, pp. 115, 117; Chase Manhattan Bank, p. 172; Franklin Institute, p. 96; Mildred E. Hardman, p. 37; INA Corporation, pp. 167, 169; John Wanamaker, p. 171; Maytag Company, p. 26; Milton Bradley Company, pp. 19, 38, 44, 45; Montgomery Ward & Co., pp. 156, 157, 168; National Baseball Library, p. 102; Nebraska State Historical Association (and from Montgomery Ward & Co.), pp. 15, 32; New York State Historical Association, pp. 54, 153; Pennsylvania Hospital, pp. 80, 83; Santa Fe Railway, p. 142; United States Lines, Inc., p. 147; Wells Fargo Bank History Room, p. 133; Zoological Society of Philadelphia, p. 183. Acknowledgment also goes to The Free Library of Philadelphia for photographs of the Centennial, the playbill, and illustrations from *Frank Leslie's Illustrated Newspaper* and *Peterson's Magazine*.

Library of Congress Cataloging in Publication Data

Hilton, Suzanne.
   The way it was—1876.

   Bibliography: p.
   Includes index.
   1. United States—Social life and customs—1865–1918
—Juvenile literature.   I. Title.
E168.H65   917.3'03'82   74-20665
ISBN 0-664-32558-0

To Christine

—a child of the next century

CONTENTS

INTRODUCTION

The more things change,
the more they are the same.
—Folk proverb

At first the year 1876 did not look as if it was going to be anything special. There were a few newspaper articles about a centennial celebration, but only the people who lived near Philadelphia were much interested in the big fair planned for the summer.

The United States of America was about to have a very important birthday. It was no longer a new nation—it was one hundred years old, and it was still healthy.

But it did have problems. A few years earlier, there had been an attempt to impeach the President himself for being dishonest. In this year of 1876 people would discover that the Secretary of War, William W. Belknap, had accepted bribes. The Department of the Treasury discovered dishonest people in their own office when they uncovered the whiskey ring scandal.

Milkmen watered down the milk. Storekeepers gouged country people with high prices. Employers did not bother to provide safety for their employees—if a man was hurt on the job, it was his tough luck. Pioneers could buy government land at ridiculously low prices just by agreeing to go west and settle on the land, but many only pretended to be settlers and instead sold their land to land companies.

There were two kinds of oil shortage. Petroleum had been discovered in Pennsylvania. The new kerosene lights were much better than lighting with whale oil. And the new petroleum did not gum up machinery as whale oil did—especially during cold weather. Many old sea captains had sold their ships and gone out of the whaling business by 1876. Whale oil was getting hard to find.

The new petroleum was not easy to get either. The oil flowed out of wells in northern Pennsylvania so fast that it could not be hauled away quickly enough. Teamsters had to carry barrels of oil in their wagons down muddy rutted roads to the railroads. Then the barrels were loaded onto flatcars. No one had designed oil tank cars yet. The only other way to get oil from the mountains was by pipeline. A pipeline sixty miles long had been built in 1874 and it carried 7,500 barrels of oil a day to Pittsburgh, the nearest large city. Armed guards had to patrol the line constantly to keep the teamsters and railroad men from blowing it up. In 1876, there were plans to build a longer pipeline that could carry the oil eastward to the Atlantic Ocean. There, ships that had been converted into oil tankers would carry the oil down the coastline.

There were problems with young gangs, but not only in the city. William Bonney at seventeen had left the New York ghetto and moved west to make a name for himself. He and his gang rustled cattle and had light trigger fingers. The name he made for himself was "Billy the Kid."

People with foresight could see a transportation crisis ahead. Cities were filling up with people so fast they needed a "rapid transit system" as soon as possible. Dr. R. H. Gilbert had a great idea for an elevated highway for New York City that could carry people from one end of the island to the other in twenty minutes or less. It would not cause any pollution—even by today's standards—nor even be bothered by ice, snow, or rain. Cars would carry passengers through tubes, propelled by "atmospheric power" or compressed air. The tubes up over the street, supported by graceful

Gothic arches, would also carry letters and packages to the post offices along the way. Since 1871, Dr. Gilbert's company had been ready to start building the rapid transit, but it would be another year before the lawmakers stopped "talking it over," and even then they did not use his ideas.

The English Channel tunnel from England to France was all ready to begin in 1876. The last test shaft had been sunk and the soundings were good. All that was needed was the money. But people had been talking about the tunnel for so many years that everyone was sick of the subject. The Queen of England began worrying about her country being invaded via the tunnel and soon the whole idea was shelved—for a while. The tunnel, now called "The Chunnel," is on again and should be completed about 1980.

There were ecology problems in 1876, too. An East Toledo, Ohio, newspaperman wrote: "The ponds hereabouts are becoming green and fragrant. They ought to dry off or better still be drained off. Whose business is it to attend to it?" Yellowstone became a national park, although hunters were still allowed to shoot everything that was not human. The city of Oakland, California, established the first wildlife refuge at a local lake.

The Suez Canal was so successful—with over 1,500 ships using it in 1875 alone—that there was talk of a new canal through the American Isthmus. Politicians argued and argued about where to put it. Nicaragua seemed to be the most likely place.

Space was in the minds of many people, since a Spanish photographer claimed that he had just taken a picture of the moon using a new system. He announced that his picture brought the moon so close that he could even see the giant trees—petrified, of course—lying all over the ground. Real scientists laughed, because the strongest telescope could bring the moon about 150 miles away, certainly not close enough to see any trees. They were very sure that the moon was a dead world with immense cracks. The seas that had once covered it had all seeped down into the cracks. There was little chance that any man would ever walk on its surface because it was so far away that "the fastest express railroad train would take over a year to reach there."

In 1876 it appeared that wars might have to end and there would soon be "suspension of arms" talks. Ships were outdated as soon as they were launched. The battleship *The Inflexible*, with armor up to twenty-four inches thick in places, had four 81-ton guns. But two Italian warships were being built with four 100-ton guns. And the newest weapon, the Krupp gun, could pierce 24-inch armor from 1,800 yards away! A children's magazine had a picture of a boy's idea of warfare in 1976—the sky was full of balloons with men shooting at each other and trying to board enemy balloons across planks.

But even though in 1876 the country had its problem people, the overwhelming majority were good people—just as they have always been. Mark Twain said that the country was full of cradles that should be kept as museum pieces, if only we knew which ones to keep. Today it is easy to look back and see which cradles had rocked important babies.

The college-age crowd (and they were not all in college) included names such as Theodore Roosevelt, Robert Peary, George Eastman, Elmer Ambrose Sperry, Booker T. Washington, and Henry O. Flippen, who would soon be the first black graduate from West Point.

Among the teen-agers could be found Annie Oakley, Juliette Low, George Washington Carver, Henry Ford, William Sydney Porter (O. Henry), Victor Herbert, William Randolph Hearst, and Anna Mary Robertson (now better known as Grandma Moses, painter).

Meanwhile, down in the grade school and toddling stages were little kids with names such as Matthew Henson (who later went with Peary to the North Pole), Carl Akeley (who was to discover a new way to preserve animals for natural history museums), Wilbur and Orville Wright (who wanted to fly more than anything), and W. C. Handy (who would start "the blues").

What kind of world did these young people grow up in? What did they do on the ordinary days and the special days? How was it to be sick or to take a trip or to go to school? This is the way it was—in the year 1876.

1

HOME SWEET HOME

Mary had a little lamp
'Twas filled with kerosene.
Mary down the chimney blew
And vanished from the scene.

—From *Frank Leslie's Illustrated Weekly,* 1876

So much for the "good old days." Life a hundred years ago was not perfect—just as life today is not perfect. But the young people who lived then were happy that they were growing up in a "modern" world. The War Between the States was over and their fathers were home again. And each week brought new inventions that made life more exciting.

By 1876 almost every home had a patent kerosene safety lamp. It could put itself out if someone kicked and overturned it by mistake. It even extinguished itself if it was dropped, instead of exploding and setting the house on fire. And when a person wanted to turn the light out, he did not even have to blow down the chimney. All for $1.25. Of course it still smelled like burning coal oil, and the slightly flickering light did tend to make people sleepy when they read at night. But the lamp was definitely an improvement.

Many modern homes had gaslights. Every teen-age girl who lived in a gaslit house was happy because she got out of the dirty job of cleaning kerosene lamp chimneys, trimming wicks, and refilling lamps. Gaslights, though, were attached to the walls or ceilings, so they could not be carried around. People still used kerosene lamps sometimes. But the new gaslights did not smell like coal oil. They smelled of gas instead.

On a cold evening when not enough fresh air was mixed with the gas or coal oil fumes, people often had headaches and doctors said either of the lights might cause all sorts of illnesses. So home life was planned around daylight. Morning began almost as soon as the sun rose.

All night long the outdoor air had been blowing through the house, especially in the bedrooms. On some windows there were shutters that kept the rain and snow from coming in while still allowing the frigid outside air through. Shutters had small slats, like venetian blinds. In the morning, the shutters were folded back flat against the outer wall of the house.

Children were taught to jump out of bed the instant they were awake. Dozing in bed, between sleep and wakefulness, was thought to be "injurious to the mind and body." So was just about everything else children wanted to do. But even if they could have slept longer, there were lists of chores that had to be done.

The 1876 home did not run by itself. Every member of the family had to help. There were no thermostats to turn up the heat when it was cold. Father or the young son shivered all the way to the cellar to stir up the coals in the furnace and add new coals to bring the heat up.

Then the family bathed—in cold water. Doctors said it was better for the health than hot water. But the real reason for cold baths was that there were no hot-water heaters. As soon as hot-water heaters were invented and put into houses, people immediately forgot the health rule and wallowed in the warm water.

The cold-water baths were not icy cold if the father or son had remembered to pump water the night before so it could be "warming up" in the kitchen during the night.

In the Eastern cities, many people had built-in bathtubs, even though most doctors called them a "humbug" and a carrier of diseases. Since no one knew what did carry diseases, doctors were perfectly safe in saying this. Tubs came in several different styles. One tub stood upright and looked exactly like a telephone booth until it was laid flat for taking a bath. Another was lined in ugly zinc and was forever bruising the elbows of big men who tried to wash in it. Some people used a "bath mat" that looked like a child's plastic swimming pool of today. It was rubber and curled up at the sides just enough to keep the water from running all over the floor. Another tub was called a "sitz bath." It was shaped like a barrel, with one side cut way down so one person could sit up inside with his feet staying outside. One traveler had invented a folding canvas bathtub to take on trips.

People who did not have bathtubs took their baths standing in their cold bedrooms. The "well-arranged dressing room for a lady" had a washstand with a large bowl and pitcher, a small pitcher and a tumbler to use for rinsing the mouth, a sponge basin, a bottle of ammonia, a hairpin cushion, and a footbath under the washstand.

The rules for taking a proper bath were strict. No boy or girl ever

When "Home Sweet Home" was in the country, there were no frills such as indoor plumbing and hot water. This South Dakota family was rich enough to have time to play croquet on a Sunday

played in the water. Bathing was serious business and had to be done quickly before the person taking a bath caught his death of cold. The bather undressed completely. Then the basin was filled with water—preferably rainwater, because it was soft enough to make the homemade soap lather into suds. First the hands must be washed, then the head and face dipped into the bowl. A boy dipped his whole head in, but a girl could wash her hair only once a week.

A guide to good health suggested the following procedure for the bath: After soaping all over, the bather used the sponge to rub the soap around. A long piece of coarse flannel was dipped into the water and thrown around behind the shoulders. The bather then held his arms in the bowl of water until he counted thirty. After that, he lowered the bowl to the floor and sat in the water until he counted fifty. He next washed his legs and feet, being careful to wash between all the toes. Before using a towel to dry, he had to stimulate the skin —"scratch" is a better word—by rubbing all over with a hair glove or a brush. This was supposed to stir up the blood and maybe help the bather get warm. Two towels were needed. One was called a "diaper" and was not what it sounds like, but a soft kind of absorbent towel. The other was a Turkish "rubber," which was like the Turkish towels of today, but was used to rub and warm the bather rather than dry him off.

Father's dressing room had many drawers in it to hold his collection of vests and pantaloons. Since most houses then did not have clothes closets, each bedroom had a large piece of furniture called a "wardrobe." It had shelves and drawers inside it to hold the clothing that is hung up on hangers today. Father also needed bootjacks to help get his boots or high shoes off at night, a boot tree to keep them the right shape when his feet were not in them, boot hooks to hang them up so the high tops would not flop over and get creased, and a bootblacking kit to keep them shiny. A social guide suggested a case with seven razors—one for each day of the week—shaving soap, a shaving brush, a small tin pot for hot water, and a package of paper to wipe his razor on.

By 1876 most city families had a "water closet" indoors. This familiar item in every bathroom today was one of the most welcome inventions. For years, people had to trot outdoors to a cold little wooden hut behind the house—no matter what the weather. The only way to avoid the cold or rainy walk was to use a jar with a lid that was kept under the bed at night and had to be emptied and washed out first thing in the morning. With the water closet inside, everyone was happier . . . except for the people who preferred "earth closets" instead. They were the nature people who felt that everything taken from nature must somehow be returned to it. They could be seen every morning carrying out their "night soil" to mix in their gardens. The water closet people also returned theirs to nature, but via a flush of water.

Drainage was very important around houses. Children seemed to get sick where the drainage was bad. Doctors knew that scarlet fever, typhoid, and diphtheria occurred more where there was bad drainage, but they still thought that smells carried the sicknesses. Later on, when germs were discovered, scientists found that they had been close to solving the mystery—but not close enough.

"A cheerful, happy, neat home is the way to keep sons from becoming fast and daughters from becoming frivolous." Parents made sure that their children were surrounded with good models to follow. Mottoes hung on every wall—from "E Pluribus Unum" worked in beads to "Home Sweet Home" embroidered in wool and trimmed with flowers and trees made of human hair. On the children's bedroom walls were pictures with morals. One, for example, showed a mother holding the rose her little son had snitched from a neighbor's garden to bring her. The little boy is looking very ashamed and worried while Mother reads what the Bible has to say about stealing.

So many city houses in 1876 were exactly alike that a running joke said a man had to be careful to count the number of houses from the corner or he might find himself eating with a strange family. Most had a central stairway leading off an entrance hall. Every house had to have an entrance hall—a place to greet guests, leave umbrellas, and remove coats. On one side of the hall was the family sitting room with the most comfortable furniture—father's favorite overstuffed chair and mother's platform rocker. A table in the center held the best kerosene lamp—bright enough so an old lady with poor eyesight could read at night.

The walls were covered with paper, but a new fashion in 1876 was to divide the walls into three parts. All around the very top of the wall was a "frieze," usually a very fancy scroll. Then came the fancy wallpaper—the fussier the better. Some lovely new styles that year showed birds singing in the woods or huge cabbage-size roses. Halfway down the wall to the floor was the "dado." It was woodwork and might include a railing around the top where mother could display her best hand-painted china dishes around the dining room walls. That year dark ceilings were the rage, but by the next year, no one could stand them. The rug was usually flowered. Thick velvet drapes hung at the windows and at some of the inside doorways, where they helped control winter drafts. Valances over the windows were trimmed with plump balls and gold tassels. On the walls, where there might still be a vacant space, there were steel engravings, mottoes, mooseheads, stuffed fish, and oil paintings in thick gold frames. But people were most careful to see that every picture hung at exactly the same height, and never were an oil painting and an engraving hung on the same wall!

The very best furniture was kept for the parlor—the room that was used only when company came. The piano, a sure sign that a family was cultured, stayed in the parlor. So did the marble-top tables, bronze statues of Greek ladies, plaster casts of famous people, potted plants, fringed cushions, the family Bible, a French forest clock with a bird that twittered on a branch when it was wound up, and all the other clues that this was a family with class.

But in the very middle of 1876, after thousands of homemakers had been to see the Centennial, they suddenly got very tired of their cluttered Victorian homes. Everyone wanted something Oriental— a rug, a vase, or even an ottoman to put father's feet on. The most impressive house from any country was the Japanese house that had no furniture in it at all. The French furniture looked delicate and elegant in a way that no heavy Victorian pieces had ever looked. Homemakers were suddenly discontented and not quite sure what to do about it.

The new furnace in the cellar was accused of breaking up families. "It is well enough to have your dwelling warmed top to

The family parlor was saved for company.
This group is playing a game called Squails

bottom and have no coals to carry beyond a furnace," warned an advertisement for an indoor fireplace. "But the furnace has done immense mischief to the family powers! It scatters members all over the house and furnishes not one attractive spot in which inmates will gather as they do by instinct to enjoy the cheery comfort of a fireside." A father had to think twice before he put a furnace in his house. It was true that every room was comfortable and the family did scatter around more. To be on the safe side—and keep their sons from becoming fast and their daughters frivolous—most fathers had a fireplace as well as a furnace.

The kitchen was in the back of the house, where the smells from the cooking could go out toward the alley instead of through the house. Kitchen smells were thought to be very unpleasant and who knew what illnesses were caused by bad odors—even kitchen ones? When the smells were too bad, the house was "disinfected" by having someone carry a plate of hot roasted coffee beans through the rooms.

Cooking was done on a huge iron range that burned coal and wood. A supply of both fuels was usually brought in every day because the stove was usually kept going all day long. The cookstove was often the housewife's most precious possession in a home that was poor. A family with a range could bake fine cakes instead of having only pound cakes for parties. Until they owned a cookstove, a poor family had to cook in their fireplace. The range fire was started with small kindling wood and then coals were added to hold the heat. Matches were made in Canada—with either blue or red tips. Irish cooks used only the blue tips, and the German cooks used only the red. The kitchen floor was plain wood, but linoleum was one of the marvels shown at the Centennial. Kitchen tables were covered with shiny cloth called "oilcloth." On one side it was like canvas, but on the top surface it was smooth and easy to clean off, like plastic. There were no enamel sinks yet—just those made of ugly zinc that were impossible to make look clean.

The kitchen was the most overworked room in the house. Most of the food was made there, as well as the staples such as the bread and butter. All the fruits and vegetables that lined the pantry shelves had been canned and put away in mason jars in the kitchen.

The kitchen was the busiest room in the house. Frank Leslie's Illustrated Newspaper *published this picture of Mrs. Goodman's kitchen, along with a few of her favorite cats*

Canning was a very hot job, because most of the foods to be canned reached the proper ripeness for canning on the hottest days in August. On other days, extras such as horseradish, relish, catsup, mayonnaise, and pickles were made in the kitchen.

Roots and herbs passed through the kitchen, too, on their way to being stored for the day when someone was sick. Each family was self-sufficient enough to have its own "doctor"—usually mother—

with a bag full of ancient remedies to cure most minor ailments. Small leaves were collected from some plants to brew up a tea or an infusion when there was sickness. In the kitchen the spring tonics were also made—to keep a body from getting sick when the weather changed.

Housekeeping helpers were manufactured in the kitchen as they were needed. Every housewife had her family formula for making ink, floor polish, silver cleaner, whitewash, rat poison, bug spray, shoeblacking, shampoo, cold cream, tooth powder, hair tonic, soap, dandruff remover, and anything else anyone needed.

Often the kitchen was the beauty parlor and drugstore for the family. Doctors said that cosmetics contained "poison that induces paralytic afflictions and premature death," and they were not far wrong. Many contained arsenic and even strychnine. So, many girls made their own cosmetics.

To remove wrinkles, a girl mixed the juice of onions and white lily with honey. Then she added melted white wax, stirring with a wooden spatula until the blend had cooled. She put it on at night and wiped it off in the morning. Presto—no wrinkles. For a few hours anyway. She made perfume with flowers and called it rose water. The smell did not last as it did in the French mixture, but very few girls had ever smelled the real French product.

Every girl hated freckles. Even though she tried hard to stay out of the sun, the detested freckles showed up in summertime. There was not much a girl could do about them except get up before sunrise and bathe her face in the morning dew. She could also sop pieces of bread in milk heated as hot as she could stand and put the bread pieces on the backs of her hands to make them white. Kept on all night (the guide does not mention how to balance the bread poultices on the backs of the hands all night), the bread would make the hands lovely and white.

Every lady wanted soft skin. It showed that she was a lady and did not have to do heavy work. But she worked very hard trying to make her skin soft. One way was to cut a lemon in half, scoop out the pulp, and turn the peel inside out. Then she whisked up the white of an egg and let it sit in the lemon peel so the oils would combine with the egg. Finally she rubbed the "lemony-egg white" over her skin. Or she could melt half an ounce of white wax with a fluid ounce of cacao and an ounce of oil of almonds. When the mixture was melted, she stirred it until it was cool, then added some barley flour to make a thin paste. After spreading it on at night, she went to sleep smelling like a macaroon. Every girl had to have pearl water for bathing. She mixed orange-flower water with rainwater, added four ounces of scraped Castile soap and a sprig of rosemary. Then it was all boiled together and put into bottles for later use.

The poor girl who could not make her hair curl had a terrible problem—which also was solved in the kitchen. She bought 5 cents' worth of gum arabic (a sweet-smelling sap sometimes used to make perfume) and dissolved it in boiling water, then thinned it down with alcohol. After it stood all night, she "crimped" her hair up in curl papers and pins and poured the potion over it. This was as "permanent" a curl as a lady could get in 1876 and it lasted all day.

Even if a girl did not learn how to do a single thing in the kitchen, she did have to learn how to serve a pot of tea to her guests in the days before tea bags and powdered instant tea. First, she brought a kettle of water to the boiling stage, but she must "never allow the water to exhaust itself by long boiling." The teapot was already waiting with boiling-hot water in it to keep it hot. When the tea water was ready, this first water was poured off and the new "quite boiling" water was poured into the pot. The tea leaves were scattered on top of the water and the lid was closed tight to allow the water to draw the flavor from the leaves. After the first cups were poured, more water was added instantly to draw more tea flavor from the leaves.

Probably the best treat ever made in any kitchen was ice cream. It took the longest to make too, because so much time passed between the moment when someone said, "Let's make ice cream" and the moment the creamy dessert was actually spooned into a dish.

First the cook made a hot custard of milk, sugar, eggs, and vanilla, and then it had to cool. This took unbearably long in summer, even when several little mouths helped by blowing. At last it was time to add the cream and put it all into a tin pail. By then, someone was chopping ice into little pieces "no larger than a pigeon's egg." The tin pail was set into a large wooden pail, and layers of ice and salt were packed tightly around the tin.

Willing helpers turned the handle. It had to be kept in motion for more than an hour. As the ice melted, more ice was brought and packed around the tin pail. After half an hour the mixture might be frozen around the edges—the first hopeful sign. For another hour the crank was turned and new ice and salt were added to keep it getting colder and colder. At last the ice cream was made. The lucky child who had finished the turning got to lick the first delicious taste of ice cream from the frosty paddle.

There were some wonderful inventions for homes in 1876. Since the only way to clean a parlor rug was by beating it with a wire beater, an inventor named Melville Reuben Bissell devised the carpet sweeper. "Even the most delicate woman can succeed in pushing it," the advertisement said, and sure enough, the revolving brushes did sweep crumbs up off the rugs. There was a new knife-cleaning machine for people who were very particular about having clean knives on their dining room tables. Knives did not have stainless steel blades and many foods made them look blotchy and rusty. A stocking darner turned out to be harder to use than the old way of darning stockings by hand. For the kitchen there was an apple corer, a potato peeler, and a corn sheller—all new gadgets that were worked by hand but saved time. The new knitting machine was an expensive gadget that not many housekeepers bothered to buy, although one could knit sweaters and stockings with it. The most important invention was not new that year, but every household needed one—the sewing machine. It worked by foot power. As the feet pumped on a treadle, the needle moved up and down through the material.

A poor family had to sew their clothing by hand. But rich families could hire a seamstress, who came and lived with the family a few weeks each year and sewed enough clothes to keep them happy for months. The new sewing machine gave many women the chance to sew their own family clothing. One woman wanted a sewing machine so badly that she walked into the Singer Sewing Machine Company and asked the price of their machine. It was $150—$100 more than she had. As she turned away sadly a thought struck her and she said, "Suppose I give you fifty dollars now and promise to pay you the rest of the money each month from the money I earn by sewing clothes?"

The manager was struck by her honesty—and also by the fact that she had a very good idea. He agreed and the first case of "installment buying" went on the record. Eventually a lady could pay as little down as $5 and take home a sewing machine.

The washing machine probably would have been invented sooner if so many women had not been eager to earn their living by doing washing—especially the Irish who came to the United States with little more than the clothes on their backs and a willingness to work hard. A large tub and a scrubbing board was all they asked. But the Triumph Rotary Washing Machine was the modern worksaver of its day. "It forces steam through the goods, then revolves in hot suds with a constant change of position, then lifts and drops the goods the same as a light pounding," said the advertisements. Next came the clincher: "With this machine, a child of 12 can do more work, and do it better, than two women by ordinary methods." The perfect accessory to the Triumph Rotary was a clothes wringer that squeezed all the water out of the clothes without catching the material in its gears.

"We have got to wash today," sixteen-year-old Ada Stowell groaned in her diary on a Monday in April, 1876. The next Monday was the same story. Monday was always washday, no matter what the weather.

"Today we washed. Mama and Papa went away and when they came back, we had the washing all done." But although Ada and her sister had wanted to surprise their folks with the job they had done, they had overlooked something. The floor was a sight!

"Papa mopped the floor after us. When he mops, he puts two or three pails of water on the floor and then scrubs and makes an awful fuss just as Grandpa used to do up to Grandma's," wrote Ada.

Ada and her mother made all their own soap for washday as well as other days. For many weeks, the family saved all their extra grease from cooking. Hard fats were used to make candles and soft fats were for soap. On soapmaking day, the fats were boiled in a large vat of water to get rid of all the salt, spices, and bits of meat.

A plunger and a tub of water were all a pioneer woman needed to get clean clothes

The newest 1876 improvement to the "washing machine" was the wringer

This helped make the soap smell better—but not much better.

Meanwhile, all the ashes from the fireplace had been put into a barrel. Rainwater from another barrel trickled through the ashes and into a smaller container. It was now "lye water." The water was allowed to evaporate "until an egg put into it will barely float." Finally the fat was heated and the lye water added gradually. The mixture was cooked and stirred until done, then poured into large pans to harden and be cut up into cakes.

"A real good soap," Ada's mother said, "would make the children's cheeks pink when they washed with it."

Brown soap was used for washday, but the soap that was almost white was taken upstairs to be used for washing people. One time Ada put geranium oil into the soap mixture before it got hard. It smelled good, but her mother said that they had no use for such luxuries and Ada should not be putting on airs. Just the same, Ada saved the last cake of geranium soap in her drawer for years just so she could smell it when she opened the drawer.

Some people who could afford to buy soap bought Castile (the finest) or Sapolio soap. Sapolio was famous because the company had hired a man named Bret Harte to write its poetry advertisements. He was already a famous short story writer, but his Sapolio poems started a whole wave of rhymed advertisements.

Color was a problem when Ada's family washed. Most dresses faded very quickly because the soap was too strong and the colors were too weak. Red hardly ever stayed red very long. Families could dye their own clothes gray, yellow, black, or brown, but the pretty colors were harder to get. Since the War Between the States, there were no longer any indigo plantations in the South, so the beautiful deep-blue color was the hardest to find. The green coloring in clothes was poisonous and caused many people to get sick. Sometimes a thick green powder would fly off a green dress when it was shaken hard.

Ada Stowell's house was on a farm several miles from the nearest crossroads store. Some days the roads were so deep in mud that the family could not get to church or to the village store where they picked up their mail and the local gossip. When the weather was bad, life on the farm was very lonely. As in most farmhouses, the

Stowells rarely used their front door. All the traffic poured into and out of the house through the kitchen and back pantry. Only strangers and special visitors ever used the front door and sat in the Stowell parlor.

But even though Ada lived far out in the country, her house was like many other houses in 1876. There were many families whose homes were not typical and who lived very different kinds of lives.

Booker Washington often told of his life in a tiny Southern cabin that was heated by a large open fireplace and cooled summer and winter by windows with no glass in them and openings between the logs large enough to let the family cat have his choice of entrances. One thing Booker liked about his house—his mother was the cook for the large plantation family and there were often good foods and smells in that room. Another thing he liked—the sweet potatoes were stored in a hole in the center of the cabin floor and covered over with boards. Booker could lift out a sweet potato and put it in the ashes to cook almost any time he wanted. The children all slept on a bundle of rags on the floor. Booker never ate a meal at a table in his young life. All the children ate like animals—getting a potato here, a drink of milk there, a scrap of bread at another time.

Laura Jernegan's home was on a whaling ship. In those days when sea captains went to sea for long times, they could take their wives and children with them. For company, Laura had only her little brother Prescott. Her mother kept her very busy with lessons and with writing in her journal every day. At eight years of age, Laura knew enough about whaling to become a whaler herself.

"It is quite rough today. But is a fair wind. We have 135 barrels of oil, 60 of humpback and 75 of sperm. We had too birds. There is one now. One died. There names were Dick and Lulu. Dick died. Lulu is going to. Prescott has got a little dog, its name is Tony. We have not seen a ship since we have left Honolulu. Prescott is playing with Papa. I am in the fourth reder and the fith righting book."

Laura's home was sailing through the Pacific waters to reach the good whaling grounds by February. Soon they would be busy with the whales, but right then her father was busy doing the million and one jobs fathers did in all homes. He put up a hammock for the children and drew a chalk line across the deck to keep the little

people from interfering with the busy ship's crew. Then he caught
five mice and gathered thirty-seven eggs from mother's hens. Later
he fixed the sink "and it runs real nice," wrote Laura. "Now he is
fixing the water closet."

At last the whales were sighted.

"When the men at the masthead say There she blows, Papa gives
them 50 pounds of tobacco," Laura wrote. "It is quite pleasant
today. the men are cutting in the whales. they smell dredfully. we
got a whale that made 75 barrels. the whale's head made 20 barrels
of oil. the whale's head is as big as 4 whole rooms. and his boddy as
long as one ship. . . . the men are boiling out the blubber in the try
pots. the pots are real large. when the men are going to boil out the
blubber, too men get in the pots and squis out the blubber and are
way up to there knees of oil."

Like most children, Laura did not think her homelife was very
interesting. Another day in her journal, she wrote: "I have been up
on deck. I can't think of much to write. I went to bed last night and
got up this morning. we had baked potatoes for supeper and
biscute. would you like to hear some news well I don't know of
any."

Elizabeth Custer did not think she was born to be a pioneer
woman. But she fell in love with George Custer, a lieutenant in the
army, and that left her little choice. Either she must live in the
nearest city with a chance to see her husband about twice a year, or
she would have to pack up the smallest possible number of articles
she would need to turn a hovel into a home and follow the army.
Elizabeth chose the latter.

When the Custers arrived at their newest post in 1875, the house
was not any different from the other army post houses they had
lived in. As usual, the windows could be raised only with a great
struggle and had to be held open by wooden props. Each room had
an old-fashioned box stove "such as our grandfathers gathered
around in country schoolhouses," Elizabeth wrote in her journal.
There were no window shades, but she hung curtains for privacy.
She hung netting in the bedroom windows and around the bed in
the hopes of outwitting the tough little Dakota mosquitoes. She
unpacked her jar of glue first and then opened the barrel that held

the few pretty (and breakable) belongings she was stubborn enough to carry with them everywhere. She was relieved to see that the two statuettes had broken in their usual places and so there would not be any new cracks. They were a pair of army scenes and special favorites of both the Custers—one was called "Letter Day" and the other was "Wounded to the Rear."

The new house was not too bad, actually, she decided. There were plaster walls. Fortunately there was no "petroleum paper" between the outer walls and the plaster—Elizabeth knew how dangerous that could be in a fire. There was no well, but a river nearby would provide drinking water. She glanced out of the window at the river and knew immediately how the water would taste—providing they waited until the sediment settled to the bottom of the bucket before drinking. Once Custer, now a general, brought her a present from his trip into the Black Hills—a jug of perfectly clear mountain water! They had saved that water for special occasions for a long time. Another time he had brought her a box of strawberries—the first she had seen in years.

There were no general stores out on the prairies where the army men were stationed. Each company of men had its own garden and there was much competition to see who could raise the best vegetables. Usually even the winners were not worth getting excited over. Once the general had brought back a huge cabbage from Bismarck and that had been reason enough to have a party. Eggs were another great luxury. Army wives had crystallized eggs that lasted a long time in a can. But since the whites and yellows were all mixed up and dried together, they did not really taste quite right. When the men hunted, they often brought home something unusual for dinner.

Strangely, Elizabeth Custer's home had more space around it than most women would ever see in their entire lives. Yet she and the other wives could never enjoy it. They could not leave the fort without guards—even to walk down to the river. All their entertainment was within the walls of the fort. They had parties and sewing bees. And there were clubs, such as the reading club, which existed only as long as the train was still running into the city to bring back new books. During the winter, the train did not run and the club had to stock up on books early or change into some other kind of club. "At least," Elizabeth wrote, "the women could not afford the luxury of disliking each other. There were so few of them they just had to get along."

What Elizabeth and the others missed most was a tree. The nearest one was eighty miles away and it had seventeen dead Indians in it. On the plains, the Indians used the few trees around as burial places for their most important people. Every newcomer tried planting trees and grass seed, but when the wind blew across the prairies, the seeds blew along with the dust and sand. Only the mosquitoes really thrived. When the ladies took their evening walk around the inside of the fort, they wrapped their ankles in newspapers, wore head nets that looked like a doll's hoopskirts over their heads, and whisked their handkerchiefs and fans through the air. Their men might hold back the Indians, but nothing could discourage the mosquitoes.

Jed Walker's family was moving to Nebraska. When Mr. Walker had heard how cheaply he could buy his own piece of land out there, with free train transportation thrown into the bargain, he could see no reason for staying in Pennsylvania, where already one farm was right up against the next farm. He convinced his family that they would have "room to grow" in Nebraska. Besides, there was no Indian trouble there—only friendly Indians. Until they could build their own home—a matter of just a few days according to Jed—the Walkers would stay with a family who had moved there the year before. The house could be as large as they wanted, because there was plenty of "building material" right on their own land.

The family had to get off the train at Lincoln, Nebraska. That was as close as the railroad came to the Walker "estate." Jed had not planned on spending so much to rent a wagon and two oxen to cart the Walkers and their few belongings the next 187 miles to where their new home would be. At least the weather cooperated. He kept thinking about that nice poem their favorite neighbor, Dr. Brewster Higley, had written. Another friend was setting it to music, but Jed could only remember the words—something like "Home, home on the range, Where the deer and the antelope play . . ." As the oxen

A family poses proudly in front of their sod house—all wearing new clothes Mama made from a bolt of material she ordered through the Montgomery Ward catalog

plodded along, Jed thought that Dr. Higley must certainly have been thinking of the plains country when he wrote those words.

The other Walkers were looking for signs that they were nearing their destination. Where were the woods? Jed had said they would have all the building materials they needed on their own land. But even when Jed stopped the wagon and pointed toward the setting sun, they did not believe they were looking at their new home. There was no home. No neighbors. Then suddenly they saw people, coming out of little hills and waving.

Jed felt a pang of guilt, but he knew his family would rally round him. In no time at all, he would have a small sod house like the others there on the prairie. And someday when lumber was cheaper on the plains, they would build themselves a real house. They would not always live in one built of dirt. Besides, it had advantages. It was warm in winter, and cool in summer. He had heard that the roof collected rainwater, like the ground, and that sometimes it rained inside the house until it dried out again. But they could get used to it. They were landowners now. He started to sing a country song he had heard a long time before:

> "My house is constructed of natural soil;
> The walls are erected according to Hoyle;
> The roof has no pitch but is level and plain
> And I never get wet till it happens to rain."

2

WHAT IS THERE TO DO?

Thus we play when our work is done,
Work is done, work is done . . .

—Last verse of "Here We Go 'Round
the Mulberry Bush" game in 1876

Playing was the last item on the list of things for children to do in 1876. They were lucky. Their parents had not been allowed to play at all, because play was considered idle. But now there were new ideas. Some very educated doctors even said that playing was good for children as well as educational.

But the world in 1876 was not ready for playing. Schools had space around them for a play yard, but only a few of them even had a swing or a seesaw. There were no radios, movies, television sets, stereos, or record players. The nearest thing to a comic book was the jokes in the almanac that was published once a year. Still there was lots to do—but only after the chores were finished.

Chores always came first and took up many hours of a boy's or girl's day. They were not just jobs to keep children busy, but necessary tasks that helped keep the household running smoothly.

Underneath the icebox was a large pan into which the melting ice water dripped. The pan filled up more quickly in summer than winter, since the icebox was not well insulated. When the pan was full, the water began overflowing out onto the kitchen or pantry floor. It had to be emptied at least twice a day, and sometimes four or five times a day. A few ingenious boys rigged up a way to get out of this chore by attaching a pipe to the icebox through which the water could drip and empty itself onto the ground under the house.

The kitchen range, if a family was lucky enough to have one, burned coal or wood. Sometimes both. Baking was done over the coals, but a wood fire was built first to get the coals started. The coal scuttle had to be kept filled so the cook could toss on more coals during the day to keep her oven the right temperature. Pieces of wood had to be split into the right sizes to use in the stove. Ashes had to be removed through the ash door of the stove before a new fire could be started. These were chores for boys.

Ashes had to be emptied from the heater down in the cellar too. All the ashes were saved for later use or else put out for the ashman, who sold them back to families for their gardens in the summertime. In some homes, the ashes were used to help make soap. Every night the fire in the furnace had to be "banked." Banking the coals meant stacking them up so they would burn very slowly and evenly during the night. In the morning, the coals were stirred up and new coals added to get the heat up in the house again.

Most city houses had water piped indoors, but many homes had pumps outside in the yard. It was usually a boy's job to pump fresh water and carry the buckets inside. After a few freezing mornings, the boy soon learned that the pump handle must be left in the up position on a cold night so it could be moved in the morning.

One of the girls' chores was to clean and trim the lamps. Kerosene lamps had wicks that were lighted each night. Next day the wicks had to be trimmed off so they would light straight across when night came again. The glass chimneys of the lamps always got smoky and had to be washed to give as much light from the lamp as possible. New kerosene had to be poured into the lamp's base every few days. By 1876 many city homes had the new gaslights on their walls, but kerosene lamps were still used as a "walking around" light.

Rich families had "upstairs maids" to make their beds. But in most families, making the beds was a job for girls. Blankets and sheets had to be aired by being hung out the window for the sun to "disinfect" them. Mattresses were turned over every day, but some of the new ones were so heavy that daily turning was impossible. At least the mattress had to be "plumped up," because after a night's sleeping, the mattress stuffing was squashed into uncomfortable lumps.

All dishes were breakable, so dishwashing was a tense job for a girl. Most mothers thought their daughters should at least learn how to wash dishes, even if there was a maid in the house. After all, the daughter had to learn every job so she could teach the maids in her own house to do them. There was a wooden bowl to wash glassware in, because the earthenware pan used for dishes might spoil the polish on the glass. After the glassware was washed, it was set to soak in cold water. Then each piece was wiped with two different towels—one for drying, one for polishing. Glass towels were never used for anything but glassware. Tea towels were used only for dishes and silver. Older towels were saved to dry the pans.

When the chores were finally finished, on a hot day the children began to listen for the iceman's jangling bells. While the iceman carried in the heavy blocks of ice, children climbed onto the back of the wagon and scooped up handfuls of the smaller chips of ice, cool and smooth to suck. Another summer entertainment in town was going down to the firehouse and talking to the firemen, who were always full of exciting stories. Country children had many entertainments that city children missed, such as playing in the hay, riding ponies, collecting chicken eggs, picking berries and apples, playing a game with old horseshoes, and sometimes swimming. For a swimming hole, no special bathing suits were needed. A boy wore old pants and a girl kept an old dress especially for swimming.

Most of the fun things to do were for boys. A girl was supposed to begin acting like a little lady as soon as she was out of diapers. She was encouraged to play with her dolls until she was a young teen-ager, because doll-playing taught her to become a mother. Even the books a girl read were not so much fun as those of her brothers. Two new books in 1876 were especially for girls. For older girls there was *The Young Lady's Book: A Manual of Amusements,*

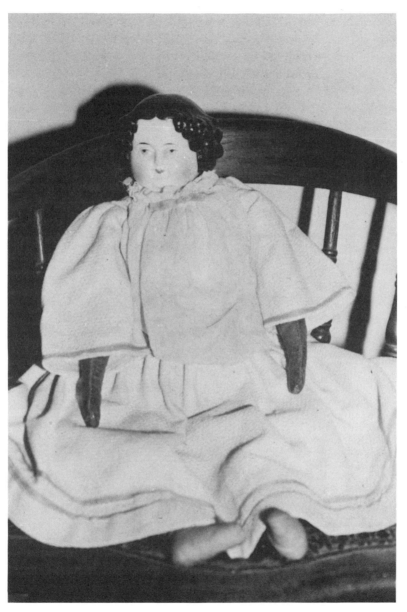

"Annie" helped teach a little girl to be a good mother in 1876

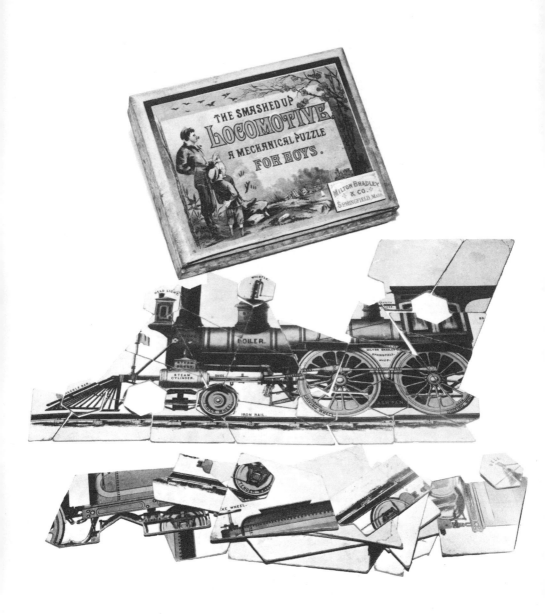

This puzzle for boys was thought to be too hard for a girl to work

Exercises, Studies and Pursuits. Meant to fill a girl's time "between school days and the much-looked-forward-to possession of a home of her own," it reminded the reader again that "idle wasting of time" would be injurious to the mind and body.

For a younger reader there was *The Holiday Album for Girls* filled with very moral little stories about children. There were Thoughtful Maggie, who helped an old lady on a train, and Eva, who was crippled but still managed to be happy. And the twin sisters Abbie and Addie, who argued like most children, but made up with each other unlike most children. And Patient Lina, another crippled girl, who taught everyone to be patient. Her name made sure the reader got the point. And Azzie, the poor girl who stole a story paper from her schoolteacher because she did not own a piece of paper with a picture on it. And naughty Ester, who would come to no good end because she stayed in bed after she had been wakened by her mother.

Teen-age girls who could get hold of "story papers" were thrown into an entirely different world from the one they lived in or the one they were going to grow up into. These stories were always about beautiful and good ladies who had dozens of servants and lived in elegant homes in some faraway land. The stories were helped along with such gimmicks as trapdoors, forged letters, disguises, and often a handsome Englishman. Providence usually intervened just in time to save the damsel from a fate worse than death. Her hero did not drink, smoke, gamble, or say bad words. No man a girl ever met could have measured up to the shining white heroes of the 1876 type of soap opera on paper.

Meanwhile, boys were reading about the glorious adventures of other boys in gold mines, on whaling ships, sailing the seven seas, and mountaineering in the Sierra Nevadas. There were many series of exciting stories for boys. One, the Great Western Series, was just new. The first volume was called *Going West, or the Perils of a Poor Boy.* The poor boy, whose name was Alexander, shortened to Sandy, had grown up in a poorhouse never knowing, of course, that he was heir to a great fortune. He does not get his fortune until he has survived the most hair-raising adventures known in books. The poorhouse is the good part. From there, things go from worse to worst as he is taken to the home of a miserable ship captain named Boomsby.

Something entirely new had been happening in children's books within the past few years. Readers were getting tired of hearing about good little children and how they were always rewarded. Mark Twain wrote a story about little Jacob Blivens called "The Story of the Good Little Boy Who Did Not Prosper." Then in 1876, he wrote *Tom Sawyer*. It was not supposed to be a children's book at all. Twain had written it to remind older people about what their world was like when they were young. Instead of getting nostalgic, most of the older people were shocked. A library in Brooklyn, New York, would not put the book in their children's library. In Denver, Colorado, a library would not allow *Tom Sawyer* on *any* shelf.

But in spite of what librarians thought might be good for them, the children wanted to hear about bad boys and girls. One book, printed first in Germany, was published in English in 1876. It was called *Max and Moritz* and had funny pictures of two dreadful little boys playing tricks. Here's how it begins:

> Ah, how oft we read or hear of
> Boys we almost stand in fear of!
> For example, take these stories
> Of two youths named Max and Moritz,
> Who, instead of early turning
> Their young minds to useful learning,
> Often leered with horrid features
> At their lessons and their teachers.

Max and Moritz were even worse than they had to be. They killed and ate the Widow Tibbets' chickens. Then they almost drowned the village tailor, put gunpowder in the minister's tobacco pipe and pinching bugs in their uncle's bed. Finally, they ended by being ground up with the corn and fed to the ducks.

Alice in Wonderland tickled the imagination and Edward Lear's nonsense poetry tickled the funny bone of many a child. *St. Nicholas Magazine* was popular, especially with boys and offered a variety of fare.

Something else was brand-new in books. Until this time all the characters in books spoke with almost perfect English copied from

British children's books. *The Hoosier Schoolmaster*, published in 1872, was the first book to be written in a local dialect. The people in this book really sounded like the people who lived in southern Ohio, Indiana, and Illinois on the north side of the Ohio River.

Not all children could afford books. The year 1876 was the one in which libraries were starting to grow and children could borrow books to read free. There were also many magazines for children. These were filled with stories (sometimes the morals were not too obvious) and also puzzles, rebuses, and riddles.

There was often a diamond puzzle. Its answers were always in a diamond shape, like this:

(1) a consonant	F
(2) a drawing	MAP
(3) an artificer in bricks	MASON
(4) a custom	FASHION
(5) a stop	POINT
(6) a word of negation	NOT
(7) a consonant	N

There were crossword enigmas too:

My first is in David, but not in Josiah.	D
My 2nd is in oven, but not in fire.	O
My 3rd is in night, but not in day.	N
My whole is a river far away.	(The river Don is in Russia.)

Or there were new charades each month:

My 1st is a boy's nickname.	BOB
My 2nd is an exclamation.	O
My 3rd is a joint.	LINK
My whole is a bird.	BOB-O-LINK

Every issue of the magazine had new jokes:

What's the next thing to a hen stealing? A cock robin (robbin').

When you see a young goat asleep, is it a case of kid-napping?

It's dangerous to go out in the woods in the spring because that's when the trees begin to shoot.

Or the one about the sign in the barber's window that read: Boots Blacked Inside. A boy asked, "Isn't that hard on stockings?"

Many children in 1876 never had a book or a magazine to read. Pioneer families traveling west in wagons had no space for books. Most Negro children had not learned to read. But some of the very best stories in this country's history were told around the campfires about legendary heroes. Every important occupation had its own "superman."

The railroads had John Henry, although sometimes this black superman was a tunnel digger, a circus roustabout, or a cotton picker. Whatever his job in the story, John Henry was the big, tough black man who symbolized the struggles between men and machines after the War Between the States.

The supercowboy from Texas was Pecos Bill. He had dropped off the back of his family's wagon and had been raised by a coyote. It was so dry one summer and Pecos Bill got so tired of carrying water from the Gulf of Mexico that he scooped out the Rio Grande River. He had a horse called Widow-Maker that had been raised from a colt on nitroglycerine and dynamite. Both explosives were still new in 1876.

Alfred Bulltop Stormalong, whose initials A. B. S. also stand for Able Bodied Seaman, glamorized the sailing man. Stormalong tales were invented by the men who could not bear to see steamships ever take the place of sailing ships. Stormalong's ship, *Courser*, had masts so high they had to have hinges on them to keep from bumping into the sun and moon. He had to order his sailors to climb the rigging to change sails six days before a storm came because it took them that long to get up top. Men had to ride horses from one end of the ship to the other.

Mike Fink was the Stormalong of the Mississippi River scene. He hated steamboats because he was the old type of boatman. Paul Bunyan was the super-lumberman from the Midwest. It would be many years before someone would begin writing down all these legendary tales. In 1876 they were just stories that traveled and grew by word of mouth.

Most children learned the "Man in the Moon" story from their nurses when they were very little. When Moses found a man gathering sticks on the Sabbath Day, he banished the man to the moon—so far away that he was beyond the reach of death. When they looked at the moon, little children tried hard to picture the man in the moon with his bundle of sticks showing on his back. The same story was told to children in many different countries. In a church in Wales, there are symbols of the orbs in heaven. One of the orbs, the moon, has a man on it with sticks on his back.

Children who lived on the seacoast or whose fathers sailed in ships often heard the story of the *Mary Celeste*.

Near the end of 1872, a British ship captain had sighted a ship heading west about five miles away from his own ship. Something about the way the strange ship's sails were set bothered him. As his ship sailed closer, he saw that one sail was tattered. When he was close enough to hail the ship, there was no answer to his calls. He sent two of his men on board the two-master that bore the name *Mary Celeste*.

The men found one small boat missing. The rigging was torn, but the ship was seaworthy. Food and water were on board. They found the ship's logbook with an entry written only two weeks before. The British captain towed the ship to Gibraltar, where detectives tried to piece together the missing parts of the ship's story.

The beds had not yet been made in the captain's cabin. The toys of his two-year-old daughter, Sophia Matilda, were in their place. A hymnbook was still on the melodeon, placed there by the captain's wife. There were clothes scattered in the crew's quarters as if the men had left in a hurry, but there were no signs that the ship had been in any storms. Today there are new theories about what may have happened to the *Mary Celeste*, but in 1876 the story was just beginning to be a legend.

There were many games for children to play in 1876—quiet games such as dominoes, parcheesi, backgammon, and checkers. Checkers were especially for girls. Chess was for boys because people thought girls did not have enough brains to play the game, though they said it more politely. *The Young Lady's Book* states: "Chess is not a game much played by ladies as it requires rather more thought and calculation than women possess." The author was a woman, too!

Some children were not allowed to play card games. Their parents thought that since cards were used for gambling, their

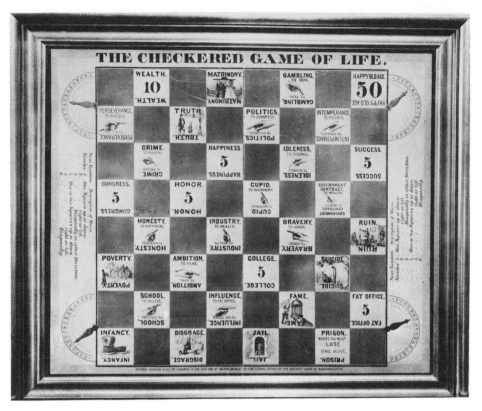

Milton Bradley's first game is still being played a hundred years later—with a few changes

children might turn into gamblers if they were allowed to play with cards. Those who were allowed to could play Old Maid or Old Bachelor or a game called "My Rose Has Budded." In the last game, each player passed one card at a time until someone ended up with all the cards of the same suit in his hand.

Almost every child had a collection of some sort. One of the newest hobbies was a stamp collection. By 1876 several countries were issuing stamps, although there were not enough different stamps yet to fill much of an album. Most had pictures of important men on them, but recently some had pretty pictures of the issuing country. These were especially popular. Today's stamp collector buys hinges to attach his stamps in a book, but an 1876 collector made his own. He bought thin onionskin paper and put a weak solution of gum arabic on one side. Next he cut the paper into thin strips and lined up his stamps on the edge of the strip, leaving a little of the sticky paper above the stamp. Finally he cut them apart with care and put the stamps in his book. Already there were counterfeiters making fake stamps, so the collector had to become an expert quickly.

The picture cards from the grocery store were almost the only color pictures a child could get. Even though the pictures advertised everything from soap to medicine, they were valued and could be "traded" with other collectors. Making object cards kept some children busy. They sewed sprays of wheat, oats, barley, rye, and buckwheat onto separate cards or attached them with thin strips of adhesive paper such as the druggist used. Object cards were always

At last it was no longer considered "sinful waste" to play with toys

good for a game when the name was put on the other side of the card. They had no limit—some were made with small shells, leaves of different trees and plants, butterflies, beetles, pieces of bark, slices of pinecones, pressed flowers, or any other item that could be made to stick to a card.

Most girls had an autograph book for friends and relatives to sign. Naturally, when a person was asked to write a line in an autograph book, he felt he must say something very important and in his fanciest writing. The composition should have a moral and take a great deal of thought.

Hattie Stowell's autograph book has this from her friend Kittie:

> May happiness be forever thine
> And peace thy steps attend.
> Receive this token of Respect
> From one who is your Friend.

One of Hattie's teachers wrote:

> When our weary task is done,
> The conflict o'er, the victory won,
> May we be found of finest mould
> As tried, refined and pure as gold.

But Hattie's boyfriends could not be quite so flowery. Nathan wrote, "In memory's casket, drop one gem for me." Richard wrote, "Lacking human wit and fame, I will simply sign my name." But when Frank was asked to sign the book, he got fresh and wrote:

> Fruit is soft as soon as ripened,
> Love and kisses soon grow old.
> Young men's vows are soon forgotten,
> Look out, Hattie, don't get sold.

It was safer to keep a floral journal—that is, a book of dried flowers. It could be almost as sentimental as an autograph book, because sometimes the flowers were from a boy or from an important walk in the woods. The flowers were dried by laying them between two sheets of blotting paper and placing something heavy on top of them, like the family Bible. After a day or two, they were ready to be put away in an album.

Not every home had a pet dog or cat. "It is not a fitting amusement for young ladies," says *The Young Lady's Book*. The best a girl could hope for, said the book, was a canary in a cage. Above all, a family should never try to keep a parrot, because parrots often learned bad words. One lady described how she finally managed to break her sailor son's parrot of his bad habits by shutting it up in a dark closet every time it said something naughty. Eventually, she said, the parrot repeated the same sentences as before, but left out the bad parts. Goldfish in a bowl were acceptable pets.

Many adults were joining clubs in 1876, so children wanted to form clubs too. The magazines for boys and girls encouraged them. Boys and slingshots were a dangerous combination, so the Bird Defenders Club was organized by one magazine. Both boys and girls were invited to join in the defense of their wild, feathered friends. One boy, though, wrote to the magazine and asked, "Is it all right for a Bird Defender to just *chase* a peacock in the hopes that some of its feathers will drop out?"

Not all fun in 1876 was quiet. Little children played many of the same games that children play today and with just as much noise. Every period in history had to have its counting-out rhymes to see who would be It. In 1876, they used:

> Intery, mintery, cutery, corn,
> Apple seed and apple thorn,
> Wire, briar, limber lock,
> Twelve geese in a flock,
> Sit and sing by a spring,
> O-U-T spells out and in again.

A shorter way was to say "Billy, Billy Burst, Who speaks first?" Whoever spoke first was It. Children made a bargain with each other by hooking the little fingers of their right hands and repeating a jingle that came close to saying a bad word:

> Pinky-pinky bow-bell,
> Whoever tells a lie,
> Will sink down to . . . the bad place
> And never rise up again.

One popular game was Fly Away, played with all the children putting their hands down on a table. When the leader called "Fly away, dove" or "Fly away, eagle," they lifted their hands and flew like a bird. But if the leader said, "Fly away, dog," they must not take their fingers off the table. The one who made a mistake had to pay a forfeit.

"Forfeits" were added to many games. Instead of being "out" of the game, the guilty one had to pay a forfeit to stay in the game. Often this involved funny or quite hard things to do. The leader who pronounced the forfeits had a long list of them to hand out. "Pay a compliment to each person in the room and do it in rhyme," or "Laugh in one corner, dance in another, cry in another, and sing a song in the last corner." A forfeit such as "Kiss a box outside and inside without opening it" took some thinking unless the payer knew he was supposed to take the box outside the room and kiss it, then kiss it inside the room. Sometimes the forfeit payer had to "perform a statue" until told he could relax, or act mute until told he could talk again. One of the hardest was to light a candle while hopping about on one foot.

Many children hated the part about the forfeits. That is one reason why forfeits are not used much anymore. George Washington Carver was a very shy little boy. One of his most unhappy memories was of his friends trying to get him to play games. He was always afraid the forfeits would include having to "buss" one of the girls ("bussing" meant "kissing," where George lived) and no boy could think of a worse fate.

Most games and things to do divided the girls from the boys so much that boys and girls rarely played together. This fitted in perfectly with the ideas for raising children in 1876. No boys wanted to be bored with playing girl types of things such as rubbing the verses off of tombstones onto large sheets of paper or collecting ferns. But most girls would have liked very much to be playing marbles, shinny, kick-the-tin-can, or mumblety-peg, in which only an expert could toss a knife over his shoulder at a target on the ground.

Most things a child wanted to do on Sunday came under the heading of breaking the Sabbath. The general feeling was that if

Sunday seemed like a long day to a child, it was because he was not having the right thoughts. "It's the Lord's Day," said his parents, "and you can make it short or long depending on whether you are trying to do what He wants you to do."

Sometimes there were jokes about Sundays in the newspapers, but still Sundays were observed quietly in almost every house. "Maria," said one pious husband in the paper to his wife, "them wicked Smiths are allowing their children to play in the yard on Sunday. Tomorrow I'll sic the dog on their chickens. The judgment of Heaven must be visited on them in some way." On another page was an advertisement for a beautiful new fishing rod for $17. "You can buy a cane fish pole for 25 cents and catch just as many fish with it as you can with a jointed one that costs $17," it read. "But you can't take it apart and slip it under your coat when you go fishing on a Sunday. And a religious outside appearance is worth $16.75 to most men."

Sunday began with going to church. Most communities had several churches. But many little towns, especially in the West, had only a few buildings large enough to hold even a small congregation. The local saloons, billiard parlors, and general stores often had to serve a devout purpose on Sunday mornings. Collection plates were not needed, since someone always had a hat that could be passed. The fine points of church collections were sometimes missed by Western characters, and occasionally the "usher" was seen taking up the collection at gunpoint. One preacher from Deadwood, Dakota Territory, left a note on his cabin door on August 20, 1876, that said: "Gone to Crook City to preach and God willing will be back by 3 o'clock." That time God was not willing, and the preacher was killed by Indians just outside of town.

Rich families often paid rent for special pews in church. It was a way for churches to make money, but it did nothing to build the character of those who attended the church. One famous minister had urged workmen to sit in the back pews because "common people didn't smell good." This made Mark Twain furious and he wrote a news column next day that said, among other things: "We have reason to believe that there will be laboring men in heaven; and also a number of Negroes and Eskimos and Tierra del Fuegans and Arabs, and a few Indians, and possibly even some Spaniards and Portuguese."

The most famous preacher in 1876 was Dwight Lyman Moody, who managed to keep many people straight in a year that was filled with prejudice against any who were different in some way—whether by their color, their jobs, the countries they came from, or their religion. He was the Billy Graham of his day. Moody was asked once to pray for all the Roman Catholics to be converted. His audience was really shocked when he said that he believed Roman Catholics were as good Christians as anyone—and sometimes even better.

After church came Sunday school. Sunday afternoons were brightened—for some people—by going calling. This was a very important ritual to grown-ups and must have been pure agony for children. They had to dress in their best clothes and have their best manners polished. Every visit had to be returned by a personal visit, so there was no end to the ritual. Callers were always received in the parlor, because this was a special occasion. Usually very nice treats were served—the kind that a child wanted to fill his pockets with, but he would not have dared take more than one. The manners he showed when he went calling could make or break his whole family.

On Sunday evenings there were more church services and afterward there were socials for the young people. For many older boys and girls, the young people's meetings were the only social event all week.

Older boys and girls had a real problem. Because the games they played as they grew up were so different, boys and girls were not used to playing together at all. Suddenly they rediscovered each other. By this time, neither boys nor girls had any idea how to behave in each other's company.

Girls had been taught to "show a delicacy of appearance, speak gently and shrink from public gaze." They hardly dared look into a boy's face when talking for fear of appearing "bold." The boys had been used to playing loud games and roughhousing with their friends, and now suddenly they were supposed to know how to treat girls. There had to be some way to get these young people to be comfortable in each other's company.

Music was one way. Singing groups were organized and groups of boys and girls met one evening each week to learn new songs. The new songs were not even very new. The only way a really new song became popular was by traveling from one party to another until finally everyone knew it. Pianos cost over $700, but usually there was one in a town or at least one at the church to accompany the singers. The hit tunes of 1876 included "Grandfather's Clock," "I'll Take You Home Again, Kathleen," "Silver Threads Among the Gold," and a new Johann Strauss waltz called "Vienna Blood."

An evening of "home readings" was another way for the nonmusical young people to get together. Usually one member of the group was selected to read aloud from a famous book—always very carefully chosen. One item in an 1876 newspaper did not make this kind of entertainment sound very habit-forming. It said: "The next of the Presbyterian young people's home readings occurs next Tuesday. If your time is not in urgent demand, you will not regret attending."

Some evening get-togethers were purely for fun and did not even try to be educational. One was a "taffy pull." Taffy is a kind of candy that needs to be pulled, after cooking, until it turns the right glossy color. Then it can be laid on a platter and cut into bite-size pieces. Another amusement was playing Acted Charades. The curtains between the parlor and the dining room were drawn in order to make a sort of stage. The host or hostess gave each guest words to act out. Each syllable of a word was pantomimed, then the curtains were pulled before the next syllable was acted. Doing things together helped to relax the young people so they could enjoy each other more.

In summer there were picnics. They required much more planning than a picnic today, since there were no foods already made up such as potato chips, pretzels (except in one small town in Pennsylvania), sodas in bottles or cans, hot dogs, or buns. Food was packed in large baskets. There were no unbreakable plastic dishes, no aluminum foil, no plastic bags. Buckets of ice went along with bottles of fruit punch. Picnickers spread a blanket on the grass and "set the table" with china plates, glass goblets, and silverware. *The*

Young Lady's Book said that picnics are for "ladies who do not have hysterics at the sight of a cow or stoutly refuse to get over a stile [a stairway over a fence] in case they should show their ankles."

Sometimes one of the picnickers took along a camera. Photography was not easy in 1876, since the cameras worked very slowly and the film was not very sensitive. Many children in photos of that time are blurred because they could not sit still long enough. When a photographer wanted to get a picture of someone looking pleasant, he did not ask his subject to say "cheese." Instead, the subject said, "prunes, papa, potato, prism." The last word gave the mouth an expression a person in 1876 thought would be appropriate for his great-great-grandchildren to see a hundred years later.

When the young people of 1876 finally learned how to get along with each other easily, they began thinking up parties of their own. A "package party" was one to raise money for some worthy cause. Each person brought a package to be sold at an auction. When young people were invited to a "pound party," they were to carry with them a pound of some useful item such as sugar or flour, because pound parties were given for new neighbors or for a newly married couple. But a person invited to a "horse fiddle serenade" carried a drum or anything that would make an atrocious noise. The serenade was held outside the house of a newlywed couple as soon as their lights had been turned off for the night. Soon the couple would give up all hope of sleeping and the wife would invite everyone inside for hot chocolate and cake.

Dances and balls were the highlights of the year. The country was full of young girls trying to talk their parents into allowing them to go to dances, since doctors could not say enough bad things about dancing. The bad air made the girls sick . . . the stylish ball dresses with low necks and short sleeves would give them consumption . . . and the rotary motion from dancing in circles was injurious to brain and spinal marrow! But most of the objection to dancing was moral. It was certainly not all right for a young man and a young lady to stand arm in arm; therefore why should it be all right for them to dance that way? Such close contact with men was bound to "suggest impure thoughts."

If they had only known, the older generation could have saved up all their worrying to do the next year. That was the year the cakewalk started—and the beginning of ragtime music that would jar everyone over twenty-five years of age. Everyone would have a chance to hear the new music, since it was also the year the phonograph, or record player, was invented!

This country schoolroom had looked this way for twenty-five years and would not change for another twenty-five

3

READIN', WRITIN', AND THOSE NEWFANGLED IDEAS

Deep is the river
Deep is the brook
Bad is the boy that
Steals this book.

—Note inside a girl's
Fifth Reader, 1876

A new schoolbook was rare—especially one with pictures in it. Students had to buy their own books, even in grammar school. After being used in school for a year, the schoolbook went home and was saved until the next child in the family needed it. Usually ten years or more passed before a newer schoolbook was published, so each book had hard use. Often the books were packed into corners of the baggage when a family moved.

"Don't forget to bring schoolbooks," the people who had gone west wrote back home to the friends and relatives who planned to follow them. Sometimes it would be a year or more before enough pioneering families could get together to build a schoolhouse and hire a teacher. Until they did, the children had to learn reading, writing, and arithmetic from parents and older brothers and sisters, or anyone in the village who would take the time to teach them.

An Iowa newspaper printed instructions for building a schoolhouse. One large enough for fifty children should be about 30′ ×

35', with a few feet added on to make a cloakroom. The cloakroom held all the coats on wooden pegs, as well as all the muddy, snowy "arctics" that children had to wear when they walked several miles to school through bad winter weather. In country schools, desks had stationary wooden benches.

The newer city schools had modern furniture. Every two children shared a bench and desk. There was an inkwell in the center for learning to write with pen and ink. A shelf under the desk held books and the kind of junk all children have always collected in school desks. The bench seats flipped up, so the children could stand at their places during the morning exercise period. Outside was a yard for recess and two little outhouses, one for boys and one for girls.

The school building was not nearly so hard to find as a teacher. Anyone would do for a teacher. One New Jersey town even employed a shipwrecked sailor. There were "normal" schools where a teacher could learn to be a good teacher, but those graduates stayed in cities, where they could earn more money with less misery. Usually a person who was able to read and to work with numbers made much more money working in a store than teaching school—especially in the country. A lady teacher had to be a "Miss," or if she were a "Mrs.," she had to be a widow. This was so that she could devote her full time to her schoolchildren. She was paid so little money that she had to "live in" with different families. She boarded with each family about a month, sharing their home and food and usually tutoring their children on her "time off."

Since teaching children was supposed to be "natural" work for women, they were not paid anything like men for doing the same job. In Maine, a lady teacher was paid $4.26 a month. A man teacher earned $35.45 a month for doing the same job.

Every state had public schools by 1875, although in some states people with many children still had to pay a little to send them to school. At first, public schools were thought to be for poor children. People were ashamed to send their children to public schools. If they had any money, they sent them to private schools. Later, the children might go to a Latin school, where they had a "classical" education and learned Latin and rhetoric. The modern idea was to send the boys to an academy, where they learned more practical subjects such as English and history. Some states, such as Massachusetts, had made a law that children must go to school at least a part of the year. The usual public school year lasted 79 days, or 16 weeks.

Not everyone had that much school though. There were still many parents who thought that school was a waste of time for girls. When a certain girl graduated from Cornell University in 1876, neighbors said, "Hmph. Wait until she has children. A woman cannot have a mind and body both. If she chooses education, she cannot possibly be a good mother."

This made things very hard for a bright girl who really wanted to learn. One girl who was not allowed to go to school decided to start a library for herself. By 1876, she had three books and had read them through thousands of times. She wrote in her diary, "My literature is a volume of Shakespeare, Dr. Gunn's Family Physician, and an agricultural report. I have read the Shakespeare till I feel my morals are damaged . . . Dr. Gunn till I am a first class physician myself . . . and the agricultural report till I can discuss stock and soil with anyone."

Ada Stowell was having the same trouble at her house in the country, except that she did not have any books to read. Her family wanted her to help on the farm, but they told her that if she had enough spare time to attend school, she would spend it better helping her aunt keep house in the village. On the tenth of June, Ada told her troubles to her diary: "Today is my 17th birthday. How awful old that seems and I don't see as I am improving one bit. Oh how I wish that I could go away to school. How I want to learn. I know I would. But here I am—a great bashful green 17-year old, almost an idiot, and no chance of ever knowing any more. O dear, how I wish Grandma had lived. She would have sent me away to school and then I should have known something. But oh I have got to rot out here. I may as well commence."

There were other objections to schools too. Some teachers had radical new ideas. One was teaching sewing and cooking to high school girls. Surely they should learn that at home. "School is becoming nothing but a mud pie factory," said the town newspaper.

Another far-out idea was the teaching of science. "Our schools are turning into natural history museums!" said the newspaper again.

Another wild idea had begun in Germany—something called a "kindergarten." Many Americans had seen one in action when they had gone to the Centennial and they wanted to try one. Eighteen children from three to six years of age were chosen from the Northern Home for Friendless Children to go to a kindergarten every day. Each child had his own garden, where he grew useful vegetables, a few flowers, and even a tree. Sometimes they played games with educational toys shaped like cubes, blocks, and cylinders. Or their teacher, Miss Burritt, taught them songs.

Most people agreed that kindergarten was not a bad idea for poor city children. Their parents paid about $1 each quarter and it was sort of a babysitting service. The teacher spent half her time helping the families, like a social worker. But most parents thought that kindergarten was a waste for children of the "upper classes."

Then there was that strange idea about gymnastics in the schools. After the War Between the States, a survey of American children showed that too many of them were suffering from physical problems that could be corrected by exercise. Also, because life was becoming much easier, they were simply not getting enough daily exercise—especially in the cities.

At first, educators believed that American children should have the same sort of rigid training that European children had. Athletics in Sweden consisted of holding a difficult position on command. In other countries, students marched in military drill. But already there was a new feeling that American children should no longer be brought up to obey just for the sake of obedience. That was not in keeping with American ideas of liberty and governing oneself. So gymnastics turned into a different kind of physical education in this country.

In many schools the exercises consisted of swinging around Indian clubs that looked like tenpins from the bowling alley. But several of the mothers began to complain that their daughters were developing muscles. This would not do at all, so the exercises for girls were designed to make them graceful. They wore Greek-style flowing dresses and danced their way to health. Very quickly

The kindergarten class at the Centennial Exhibition showed parents that little children could be taught without damaging their brains

American students made it known that they did not like calisthenics at all, but they did like sports. Sports started in college and filtered down into the high schools within a few years.

In primary and grammar schools (grades 1 through 8), the children exercised with a "wand." Each child had his own wand, which he waved around, making patterns in the air and developing his muscles.

Public high schools were brand-new. There would be no junior highs for many years yet. Most children never went beyond the eighth grade, because only the wealthy children could afford to go to academies and college. A typical academy or boarding school cost $50 for board and tuition. The charge for board in 1876 included doing the student's washing, making his bed, and supplying the fuel he was likely to use for warmth and light. Each pupil took to school with him his clothes, sheets, blankets, towels, and napkins to use at dinner. The price of college was even worse. Harvard cost $150 a year, but most parents were warned that their son would have spent $1,000 before he completed his four years. Only the rich could afford the luxury of higher education. At least that was the way it had always been until 1874.

Then the State of Michigan decided that money for high school should come out of public funds. There was a court battle and the court decided that when boys and girls were educated, everyone benefited. Therefore, it would be legal to use tax money to run high schools. Young people could then have twelve years of free education. The idea spread quickly to other states.

There were still no laws to make a child go to school if his mother thought she could teach him better at home. An 1873 medical book advised a mother to keep her child at home as long as possible. Then he would not be "contaminated by naughty children, for in every school there is a great mixture of the good and the bad, and a child is unfortunately more likely to be led by the bad." The doctor also reminded mothers that a child's brain was apt to be overworked by going to school.

Those are not the only children who did not go to school. In the Northern states, Negro children went to school with white children —if they could afford to. But most black families in the North were very poor and they had to have the money their children could bring home from their factory or coal-mine jobs. Some cities had schools at night that were filled with Negroes from ages six to ninety-six who wanted to learn to read. There had been rules on the Southern plantations about not teaching slaves to read. A few white owners had taught some of their black workers to read anyway. But a Negro who had learned to read knew better than to talk about it. There were terrible stories about white "night riders" who thought educated Negroes were too uppity. The black people had good

The bronze statue of The Freed Slave *at the Centennial was a popular sight, but it symbolized a freedom most black children did not yet have—the freedom to attend school*

reason to be afraid of them. When the slaves were freed, very few of them had had any education. So when the first schools were opened for black people, they were packed. Over four million in the South alone wanted to learn. Most of their schools had nothing except a few old books given to them by groups of white people who wanted to help. Sometimes the local newspaper was the schoolbook. There was no money for pencils, pens, or paper. There was no money to pay a teacher in most towns, and very few black people had had enough education themselves to be teachers.

George was very disappointed in his first teacher. He had grown up with a white family, the Carvers, since the night his mother had been stolen by some night riders. Now he was old enough to learn to read, and he knew he could learn. Mrs. Carver had given him an old Webster's blue-backed spelling book and he knew every single word in it. There was a school nearby, but that school was only for white children. The one for black children was eight miles away. It was an old tumbledown cabin with hard wooden benches for the seventy-five children to sit on. But it was the teacher who upset George. He was a Negro, and George thought that he must be a very smart man. Within a few days, George was taught that because he was a Negro, he could never become famous or rich as he had always dreamed. Worst of all, his teacher was ashamed of being a Negro, and that had never even occurred to George.

School began early in the morning in the North and in the South. Long before the children arrived, the teacher had aired out the room. Now the heating stove in the center of the room was crackling with a warm fire. The youngest children sat nearest the fire. The room was not to be warmer than 68°, although if the weather outside was freezing, it was all right to allow the room to reach 70° for just the first half hour. The windows were large and there were no window shades because the pupils needed the daylight to see their books.

School always began with a prayer, and some teachers added a song. The song was probably not "The Star-spangled Banner." The national anthem had not been chosen, but everyone had a favorite—"Hail Columbia," or "The President's March," or "John Brown's Body." But there was much to be said for "Yankee

Doodle" as a national anthem. When the peace treaty had been signed at Ghent many years before, the national airs of the countries involved were being played by a band. But when the American ambassador was asked for his national anthem, he said there was none. And the only American tune anyone in the diplomatic group could hum was "Yankee Doodle," so that was the song the band played for the United States.

The Pledge of Allegiance was still twenty years in the future, but each school had a flag—which would very soon be outdated. It had thirty-seven stars on it, but sometime during 1876 artists would have to think of a new way to arrange the stars because Colorado had just become the thirty-eighth state.

The children were of all ages in a one-room schoolhouse. Larger schools with more classrooms were "graded," but even then not all the children in one class were the same age. Instead of moving along from first grade to second, then to third and to fourth, a child stayed in the primary department of grammar school until he could pass a hard exam given by the secondary department teacher. He could not go into the secondary grade until he had completed the Second Reader, learned the multiplication tables to 12 times 12, learned addition and subtraction, could multiply using two figures as multipliers, finished half the spelling book and all of the primary geography book, and learned penmanship on a slate. Writing with pen and ink came in higher grades.

The primary reader's first lesson was the alphabet. After that exciting beginning came real "reading" and this was page two of a typical primer:

O	go	so	go
So	go	O	go
Go	so	go	go

How did the teacher teach this first inspiring lesson? Each child read one word. Then the first child read one line. Then on to the next child, who read a line. This way, the teacher's instructions said, the sight of the words would grow so familiar that the children would recognize each of the words the next time they saw it. After more lessons that read: "Lo ho no, Ho lo No, no lo ho," the children reached their very first two sentences: "Ho ox go on," and the equally thought-provoking "O go or I go ox."

The teacher's book said that maybe a child would get bored with this lesson, but the teacher would be well prepared for the little rebel who did not care much whether the ox goes or no. Here is what would happen, the instruction book warned:

"I cannot do it," says the child.

Then the teacher will say, "What? Did I hear right? You cannot do it?"

Most children will go back and try again at this turn of events, but the book warns that some children can be very bad. The child might say, "No, I cannot do that" again.

In that case the teacher has only to say, "I am extremely sorry. I did not think you would be low enough to let anything conquer you. I took you for quite a different type of person!" Everyone in the room snickers behind his book and the child slinks back to his seat.

The children who had reached *Monroe's Fifth Reader* were way beyond the ox. They knew how to read quite well and it was time they began to work on their "reading aloud." By now they had all heard townspeople "give readings" on special occasions such as Memorial Day or the Fourth of July. Whether they were bored or impressed or giggled all through the reading, they were then about to learn to do the same thing. First they would find out that they must not slump while standing and must not sit in a slouchy manner. Their lungs had to be able to suck in large breaths of air and let it out slowly.

" 'Rousethee upO wastenotlife in . . . ,' " drones Johnny.

"Oh no! NO!" wails the teacher. She has just finished leading her class in a daily round of "Ee-ah-oo, ee-oo-ah, ah-ee-oo, ah-oo-ee" to improve their articulation. Now it is time to work on slides and inflections.

" 'Rrrrrouse thee UP!' " she corrects, with the word UP sliding upward gently. " 'O waste not life in fond delusions!' And then, John—watch the last part: 'Be a SOLdier! Be a HEro! Be a MAN!' "

The lesson for the day ended with the class trying out different pitches of voice.

"All together now, and remember, a high lilting voice."

" 'Cry Holiday! Holiday! Let us be gay!' "

Over and over the class tries to lilt. Then they practice the low, round tones of the next verse.

> " 'Hark! from the battlements of yonder tower
> The solemn bell has tolled the midnight hour.' "

The Fifth Reader group would progress further this year when they learned the proper way to thump on their chests, raise their hands high, and wallop the podium with their fists. All these attention getters were necessary before there were microphones in order to keep the audience beyond the sixth row awake or to keep from being drowned out by someone who could speak louder and more forcefully. In a few years, this group would be ready for debating.

Debating is an art, but it was also an evening's entertainment in 1876. First a topic was chosen. Resolved: Fire is more destructive than Water, or Resolved: True beauty is to be found in Nature rather than in Art. Members of each team spoke in turn and made their points for their own argument. Then after Team One heard Team Two's arguments, it had a chance to argue the point further. The winning side was decided by the audience, which voted by clapping. Debating was almost always won by the cleverest speaker, who could convince his audience that black was white if he wished.

Art was another new subject that some radicals thought should be included in school. Art courses were added to the curriculum about 1876. Girls were supposed to paint pictures of flowers. To make them feel better about not painting what they chose, they were told that only girls could paint flowers just right.

A sample drawing lesson sounded like this: "A simple line drawing is a thin mark from one point to another. Lines may be divided as to their nature in drawing into two classes. One: a straight line which are marks that go the shortest road between two points, and Two: A curved line which are marks which do not go the shortest road between two points." Only the most dedicated art lovers could go on with art after that beginning.

"A new era has dawned," said Edward Brooks's *The New Normal Mental Arithmetic*. The "new math" of today is not so new after all.

Professor Brooks had tried his system on students long before he wrote the new math book in 1873. All the teaching was done by question and answer. Here is a sample:

"What is the sum of 28 and 37? The figure on the right is a unit; the one on the left is a ten. 8 units and 7 units are 15 units, or 1 ten and 5 units. 2 tens and 3 tens are 5 tens which, added to 1 ten and 5 units equals 6 tens and 5 units, or 65."

Parts of the mathematics book would stump children today. Who knows what an eagle is? It was a ten-dollar gold piece. What is a gill? a furlong? How many furlongs in a mile? What is a perch? (No, it was not a fish.) What is a rood? How many roods in an acre? What was a scruple? or a dram? or a pennyweight? Generation after generation simplifies terms and measuring units.

Children ran away from school, but when they did, they were in real trouble. When parents in 1876 decided that they could not manage their children, they put them in a reform school. This was usually called an industrial school and was guaranteed to turn a lazy boy into a very industrious one, provided he did not escape. Any girl who ran away from home could be sent to an institution until she reached the age of eighteen simply on the word of any two respectable inhabitants of the town *where she was found!* This was called "rescuing her from a life of crime and shame." Any two directors of the institution could then discharge her "for sufficient reasons," which included her family showing up and claiming her. But there were no telephones for calling home. The best a girl could do was beg for some paper, an envelope, and stamps and write to her family for help. In many cases, she could not write, and they could not read. If she stayed in the institution, the directors could bind her to service to a family who wanted a servant girl.

One reformatory for "neglected, vagrant and viciously inclined young girls from 8 to 16 years old" was in Connecticut. There the girls were trained by living in one of two family houses, each with forty "children." A matron was in charge of each house. Her assistant was a teacher who was in charge of the schoolhouse where the girls spent their afternoons and the sewing room where they spent their mornings. Each girl must perform her duty for the day "promptly and thoroughly." If she did not, she was punished by having no amusement and no favorite foods, and by having to perform "some irksome duty." There was solitary confinement and worse for a girl who was a real rebel. The matron complained that the girls were being let out of the home at too tender an age when they reached seventeen. Besides, she told a committee in 1876, she needed the older girls to do the hard work. They were just starting to be useful at seventeen.

The boys who lived at the state reform school were from ten to sixteen years of age. Their parents had to pay $3 a week for their keep, and they had to stay at least nine months. They worked $6\frac{1}{2}$ hours a day and went to school for $4\frac{1}{2}$. That gave them about a half hour a day for "amusement." If a boy used that half hour for daydreaming (perhaps thinking of escape?), he was not being reformed enough.

A father who could not cope with a difficult young fellow actually thought he was doing the boy a favor by sending him to reform school where he would "learn to be good." The Michigan State Reformatory claimed it was too late to send them a boy at ten years of age. "Send them at eight," they said. "Then maybe we can reform him in time." Most boys stayed two to three years. Often they had no homes to go to and no one who would take them in for fear they were "bad boys." Brooklyn, New York, had a Truant Home for boys who did not want to go to school. During the years they spent there, they were definitely not truants.

Some of the children had actually committed crimes when their fathers had them sent to reform school. They may have stolen an apple or a loaf of bread. The next largest group were listed as "incorrigible." Some of them had said bad words. In one school only one boy was there for robbery, one for killing an animal, and six for being vagrants. Most of the boys had no fathers. Whether they had been picked up for playing hooky, using profane language, or using tobacco, they were treated as criminals.

The reform schools had very few Negro children. When black children got into trouble, they were sent to real prison with the real criminals. The excuse the reform schools used for not taking black children was that "their health would suffer under the diet and temperatures that suited white children." No one ever inquired whether the Negro child's health was suffering in prison.

Orphans were not much better off. Orphans included children whose parents were alcoholics, in prison, sick, in the poorhouse, insane, or just divorced with neither parent able to keep them. These children slept in one room with twenty iron beds. Each child had a closet or a box to keep his worldly possessions in. He could stay in the orphanage until he was twelve. After that, he was sent out to work as an indentured servant.

One orphan home in Buffalo, New York, really made people feel that they had done an orphan a huge favor by sending him there. It had a drum and bugle corps for the boys. The children had swings and balls to play with and there were strips of rag carpeting between their beds. School was dismissed at 3 P.M., and the girls were allowed a whole half hour to play before they began sewing school.

San Francisco had a very large Oriental population—families of the Chinese laborers who had helped build the railroads. When the railroads were finished, many people wanted to send the Chinese back to China because they were willing to work for such low wages that they were putting many white men out of work. Riots were increasing, and the importing companies that had brought the families over were not going to pay for their return. Meanwhile, nearly seven thousand Oriental children wanted to go to school. A Chinese mission school taught many—along with their mothers. Mornings were devoted to reading and writing, but in the afternoon the class sewed to help support the school.

But not everyone of any race could go to school. So other ways of learning soon turned up. Itinerant teachers moved from one small town to another, teaching their little specialties. Before the students discovered that their teachers did not know very much about a subject, the itinerants moved on to another town. In this way, women picked up such talents as painting roses on pottery, writing poetry, and even operatic singing.

"Culture" did not often get to small towns. When it did, the local newspapers made sure everyone knew. "The Leslie Concert Troupe came for two weeks," said the paper of Blue Earth, Minnesota. "They taught vocal classes to sixty and instrumental to twenty.

Professor Leslie learns them in six lessons to read music so that by practice they can make themselves singers." Whether or not Professor Leslie succeeded in improving the quality of music in Blue Earth, Minnesota, is not known. He left town in two weeks.

Some small towns were lucky enough to have libraries. But they did not have well-trained librarians who knew how to arrange the books so they could be found readily. There were no library schools yet to train librarians. And there was no system for storing the books

Many older people who never had a chance to go to school learned to spell at spelling bees or attending classes taught by traveling teachers

on the shelves until 1876 when Melvil Dewey originated the Dewey Decimal System. The same year, the American Library Association was founded to make sure that every town needing a library had a chance to start one. The association also turned the librarian's job into a profession with higher standards and better education requirements.

For a long time, people had been saying that the schools should teach boys how to make things with their hands. By 1876 so many students lived in cities that most boys no longer knew how to build a table or repair a chair. But no one knew how such a course could be taught. Then came the Centennial Exhibition and to everyone's amazement the Russians had a beautiful display of articles made by boys of high school age. American teachers started to plan an industrial arts course the very next year.

One of the few places a girl could learn to be a nurse was at Bellevue Hospital in New York City. She had to devote one year to learning her profession, then promise to stay on the second year and help train other nurses. For the first month, she would be a probationer. Next she became a pupil nurse and was paid $10 a month. She learned to care for blisters, burns, sores, and wounds. She helped the patients in many ways, but along with the interesting duties came the dull jobs that were hers to do just because she was a woman. She had to learn to cook for the sick and even to make her own bandages. The work was very hard and the hours were long. At first she could nurse only women and children, since that was "natural" work for women.

There were two service academies in 1876. The U.S. Military Academy at West Point had been in operation for many years. But the Naval Academy at Annapolis, just past 30 years old, was having problems. Its instructors had all been trained on sailing ships, while its young cadets felt the Navy should be training with more modern steamships. The dilemma would last for years. Meanwhile, the Revenue Cutter Service, which spent its time rescuing people from drowning after shipwrecks along the coast, was about to start its own academy with nineteen men who passed an entrance exam. Years later this service became the U.S. Coast Guard.

The Government owned a great deal of land and was giving some away in each state. The purpose of each grant was for a state agricultural college to be started so that young people from the state could learn farming. In 1876 people still felt that it was a mistake to allow so many farmers to move to the city. It had not become apparent yet that many new inventions were making it possible for fewer farmers to feed all the people in the country.

"How about a college on a steamship?" suggested one of the more radical radicals. But he was laughed down. It would be much smarter, many said, to have a railroad college. Would that be the education of the future? People, then, thought that it might be. A train could hold one hundred students, each of them paying $1,000 a year—in advance, in case they left the train somewhere along the route. A baggage car would hold the kitchen and storage rooms. The second car would be a restaurant. In the third car would be the "grand temple of learning," lecture room, library, and a president's office. The fourth and fifth cars would be Pullman Palace cars and serve as the dormitories. The students would spend their four years touring the United States, which by 1876 stretched from coast to coast.

4

GETTING SICK
AND OTHER CALAMITIES

No matter what ails you, one will do you good.
—Advertisement for a medicine in 1876

Elizabeth was sweeping the sidewalk in front of the house when she happened to look up at the roof of the veranda.

"Oh, no!" she gasped.

She ran closer to the porch and took another look. Unfortunately her eyes were not playing tricks on her. Elizabeth dropped the broom and ran into the house.

"Mrs. Stevens! Come quick!"

Mrs. Stevens was the mother of three children. She was accustomed to dropping everything and running quickly when she heard shouts like that. In a few seconds Elizabeth had pulled her to the front stoop where she could look up at the herb growing on her roof. Its leaves were thick and juicy-looking. The pink blossoms were ready to open. By now Elizabeth was pale and moaning.

"It's a houseleek . . . a sure sign of death." The hired woman wrung her hands in despair.

"But, Elizabeth, it's only a plant." Mrs. Stevens was not

superstitious. "There must be some way to take it off the roof."

She patted Elizabeth on the shoulder. The old woman brightened. If the houseleek could be removed—every speck of it—before the pink flowers bloomed, disaster might be avoided.

Elizabeth ran to the cellar for a box in which she could put every last piece of the plant. She had to be careful not to drop the least bit on the roof, where it could take root and grow again. Then the pieces must be destroyed completely. The hired man brought the ladder and soon the job was finished. Evidently Elizabeth was very careful, for the diary Mrs. Stevens wrote does not mention any calamities for the year 1876.

So many bad things could happen to a family that no one wanted to take any chances. No one was quite sure what caused sickness or why so many children died before they had a chance to grow up. The few doctors who believed that diseases were caused by something they called a germ were not able to make anyone listen. Some people, like Elizabeth, found it easier to blame sickness on a superstition, such as the superstition about the houseleek. Others had their favorite ways to keep their children well.

A careful housewife watched the flies that collected after meals on her dining room table. She had learned that when flies rubbed their feet together, it was to get off the tiny animals that clung to their legs—animals so tiny that a doctor had to see them through a microscope. Then the flies ate these tiny animals, which were poisonous to human beings. No smart housewife would have thought of swatting the flies that did such a good service. If the flies were skinny, she could relax. But if they were fat, she knew they were getting fat from eating so many tiny animals that came from impure air—the very air in her house! The idea that the flies might be dropping germs on the food in her dining room never even occurred to her. There were no "germs" in 1876.

No one knew about vitamins either. Mothers seem to sense that after a long winter it was important to fill their children with green vegetables. Pioneer families found that they had all the symptoms of scurvy after living on dried foods and salted meats all winter. The children were sent out to gather the first wild greens they could find in March or April. Usually they came home with dandelion greens.

They could not have found a better source of vitamin C, but in 1876 people knew only that dandelions taste sweet in early spring. They had also noticed that soon after the fresh wild greens appeared at the table, the symptoms of scurvy began to disappear. Sea captains had known for centuries that certain foods had to be given to seamen to keep them from getting sick. But no one in 1876 knew that it was the vitamins in the food that did the trick.

Another mysterious disease was common too. The victims became tired, nervous, and pale. Then red blotches began to show up on their skin after they had been out in the sun. Because they felt tired, they ate even more of the sugars and starches they had been eating too much of in the first place. Soon their tongues got red and swelled. Their throats started to burn. Some even went insane. The disease was well known and had a different name in every part of the country. The local cure was to feed the victim plenty of red meat and yeast instead of starchy foods. These people had pellagra and needed niacin, one of the B-complex vitamins.

Many other troubles bothered people because they did not know about vitamins. Eye troubles and blindness were common complaints with grandparents who had managed to live beyond their average life span of forty years. Their teeth fell out and their gums were often sore and painful, but they thought it was just a natural part of growing older. Children did not grow as tall as children do today. Nervous ailments were more common. Cracked lips became infected easily. Many babies had rickets and grew up with crooked legs. Their parents thought they had inherited crooked legs from them, but they also had had rickets. And they had been told that rickets came from sleeping on feather beds! All sorts of skin diseases were common in 1876. And all because no one knew about vitamins.

The methods that mothers used to keep their children from being sick were almost worse than being sick. Some people put their faith in long woolly underwear that began to itch after one slept in it for a few weeks. Once woolies were put on, people thought it was risky to take them off until late spring. Some refused to bathe because they felt that the body formed some sort of "protective coating" that kept one from catching colds in the winter. A bath would wash off the coating. If the pores were opened by washing with hot water, minute objects in the air could enter the body and make it sick.

"Button to chin till May be in; never cast a clout till May be out," warned the grandparents. Casting a clout meant taking off some of the swaddling clothes. Spring was time for grandmother's tonic too. Sulphur and molasses was supposed to purify the blood. Some families used spruce beer and birch tree sap, doctored up with the family's inherited recipe, of course. Most spring tonics were really laxatives that "cleaned out" a child's body. The idea was that if any "minute objects" happened to have gotten inside him from impure air, they were sure to be swept out along with everything else.

All spring tonics had one thing in common. They tasted horrible. "Just hold your nose and you won't taste a thing," said Mother. But the taste was strong enough to penetrate. Besides, most children knew that the only reason for holding their noses was to keep the right hand busy squeezing the nostrils so it could not be used to push the spoon away.

Though all families had their own medicine recipes, they were willing to try something new. A person could not read through a list of the "symptoms" cured by a patent medicine without discovering he had one of those symptoms. While he might not have alarming problems such as hair falling out and pimples, almost everyone could say he had "confused ideas, low spirits, or an absence of muscular efficiency" on some occasion.

Every general store carried shelves of patent medicines in the form of balms, balsams, compounds, cordials, cures, drops, elixirs, emulsions, liniments, mixtures, oils, pills, sarsaparillas, syrups, and waters. There were no laws regulating medicine at all. Any man could call his medicine a "cure" though it had never cured anything. A medicine maker could call himself "Doctor Smith" when he had never so much as walked past the door of a medical school. He did not have to tell what was in his bottle of "cure." In fact, if it was a secret formula, so much the better. The very same medicine sold to people was also sold for horses or cows.

The local grocer was the biggest patent medicine pusher. He passed out copies of the latest almanac (published by the patent medicine people) as if they were rare copies of first-edition books. On his walls were beautifully colored posters and small trade cards in four colors that the children could take home with them for collections. One unforgettable poster shows sickly, hollow-cheeked children on one side of the picture. On the other side, they have been miraculously restored to health by taking only one bottle of Mrs. Winslow's Soothing Syrup.

Unfortunately, Mrs. Winslow's product was full of morphine. The makers knew that, but it did quiet the children so nicely! They called it the "Florence Nightingale of the Nursery" and filled their advertisements with letters from grateful parents. It would be many years before the parents discovered that they had turned their babies into drug addicts. Many other medicines contained ingredients that were just as dangerous, such as laudanum. Today we call it opium.

The people of 1876 could thank the patent medicine companies for starting billboard advertising too. Many people called the year the Age of Disfigurement. Others called it "obscenery." During the construction of a new post office in New York City, a board fence was built around the site. A medicine company rented the space and painted its advertisement on the fence. Soon the makers of all sorts of medicines were decorating the countryside with their signs. There was no kind of regulation. A farmer might wake up one morning and find that the side of his barn said "Try Plantation Bitters," and almost before the paint was dry, another advertiser might cover it over with "Who has not heard of BUCHU?" A sign hanging way out over Niagara Falls reminded tourists of "Herrick's Pills" and "Lightning Oil." All across California were yellow signs reading "Merchants Gargling Oil." Travelers yearning for their first view of Yosemite saw instead a sign reading "Yosemite Bitters Good for Belly Ake." Things began getting out of hand when one promoter bought a Mississippi River stern-wheeler and painted his advertisement on the side in twelve-inch-high letters. Another covered an old steamship with a sign advertising liniment and sent it over Niagara Falls.

Not all the patent medicines were full of dangerous drugs. Many were full of alcohol. One vegetable drink for delicate girls was popular with farmers in a state that would not allow alcohol to be sold. It was 18 percent alcohol. Religious newspapers were filled with articles against drinking liquor, yet their back pages were filled with advertisements such as "Vegetable Pain Killer, the constant companion and estimable friend of the missionary." The companies that made alcoholic medicines even marched in temperance parades and donated money to the cause. They said alcohol was bad, but used as a medicine it was perfectly all right. The worst part was that parents had no idea they were giving their children liquor, because medicine makers never told what was in their cures.

Even though parents tried hard to keep their children well, they did not always succeed. All sorts of simple problems plagued children in 1876. They had lice in their hair. For that, they rubbed camphorated oil into their scalp and left it on a whole day. They got beestings and cuts, but if Papa chewed tobacco, he could apply some of the tobacco juice to them to make them better. Or let the dog lick them. Stepping on a rusty nail was dangerous. A careful person picked up the nail, greased it, and carried it in his pocket to prevent sickness. The storekeeper of the general store was the man to see if a child was bitten by a mad dog. He had a "madstone" that had been taken from the stomach of a deer and that supposedly had made the deer twice as hard to kill. A madstone was a hard object covered with calcium, but it was smooth and round from being in the deer's stomach for years. One day Abraham Lincoln had taken his son Robert to the store to use the madstone. The stone was touched to the wound. If it did not stick, the dog was not rabid. If it stuck, the dog had rabies and the child would probably die. People thought there was no point in seeing a doctor because no doctor had ever cured rabies.

The most common ailment was an upset stomach. Country people called it "feeling wamble-cropped." But an upset stomach could be anything from a tummy ache to a symptom of something much worse. It was hard to describe too, mainly because nice people never used the word "stomach." Here's the way Anna Lindsay described hers to her cousin Olive:

"I came home from school with a terrible headache. I layed down. Did not eat any supper. After I got a little better, went to the sideboard and took out a piece of jelly cake very careful not to let anyone see me eat it. The next day I had to go to bed and layed there two weeks. It was a Billious Attack with a very high fever. It seemed to me I had mustard plasters all over. But the hardest thing was to do without eating. I don't believe I ate more than half a slice of bread in those two weeks. But I am well now and have been for three or four days. Pa doesn't allow me to go out yet. I do not like to be sick very much."

When a child had a cold, his chest was rubbed with coal oil and lard—a hideous-smelling combination—and covered with a piece of old flannel. His throat was rubbed with camphorated oil and a smell like moth crystals stifled his nose. His feet were plunged into a mustard footbath with water as hot as he could stand it "to draw the cold downward." Fighting his cold from within was a large dose of castor oil, a thick oily liquid that had to be swallowed again and again before it went down the throat. (In those days it was not tasteless like today's castor oil.) Syrup of cherry bark every hour and syrup of honey and alum in between times were supposed to cure hoarseness. Since miasmas (or bad smells) were supposed to cause sickness, one had to disinfect the room by carrying a plate of hot roasted green coffee around. When a child was very sick, his mother burned sulphur in the room and hung a sheet at his door to "keep the sickness from going outside the room."

The sick child got special foods to eat such as gruel, milk toast, or beef tea. Mother made many kinds of infusions. An infusion is made by boiling herbs, barks, or leaves in water to make a tea. Then the patient had to drink the tea no matter how awful it tasted. Pills were made at home, too, by adding a little flour to the medicine recipe. Pills were made "about the size of a pea."

For aches and pains, there was always the mustard plaster. Ground dry mustard was wet with cold water and stirred until it made a smooth paste. The paste was spread on a piece of newspaper double the size of the mustard patty and then enclosed in a piece of cloth. The cloth was folded carefully so that none of the mustard could leak out and burn the child's skin, and the plaster was placed on the patient's back—if the pain was in his chest. It stayed on about seven minutes. It felt warm and the skin underneath turned a bright-red color. The plaster could really make blisters if it was allowed to stay on too long.

Meanwhile the poor patient got weaker and weaker as his body fought the fever. In those days there was no penicillin or other antibiotic to help reduce a fever fast. The child just got hotter and hotter until the fever "broke." By that time, the patient had hardly any strength left. Getting better took a long time.

Sometimes a child got so very sick that his mother's kitchen medicine just seemed to make all his symptoms worse. After all the "doctors" in the family had finished trying to cure him, the real doctor was sent for. Doctors had a very hard time building up their reputations as "healers" when they were not even called to see a patient until he was almost dying.

That was not the only reason doctors had bad reputations in 1876. No money was spent on research and when a dedicated doctor made a discovery in a small town somewhere, no one believed him. In the whole country in 1870, there were only fifty microscopes that were any good. Then there were all those patent medicines that supposedly had been made by "doctors." People who found that Dr. X's patent medicine did not work were not likely to trust any doctors. There were very few medical schools. Most doctors had never even seen one. A young man became a doctor by being apprenticed to a doctor in his town until he learned all he knew. Then the doctor wrote a letter of recommendation for his young "graduate" and a new doctor went into business for himself. The real doctors had a hard time learning all they should know. They even had to pay for the privilege of following a well-known doctor around the hospital to see patients with unusual sicknesses.

When the doctor arrived at the home there was only one thing he could do that the others had not tried. "Let's get some of that bad blood out," he would say and bring out his bottle of leeches. The doctor believed that the body replaced its own blood as fast as it came out. The new blood made by the body would be good, so the idea was to let out some bad blood to make room for the good. The ideal way to draw it out was by using leeches.

Children were frightened of leeches, but usually by the time the

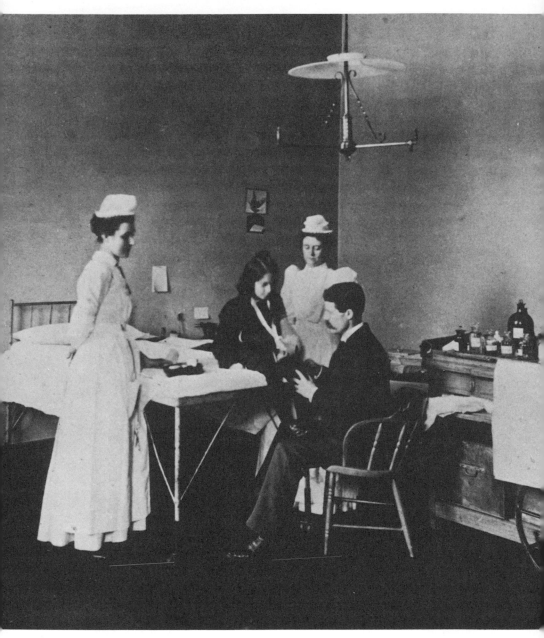

Many doctors in 1876 never saw a medical school. A medical "practice" really was "practicing"

doctor came, they were so sick they did not really know what the doctor was doing anyway. A leech looks like a very fat worm about a half inch to four inches long. It attaches itself to the skin, bites a tiny hole, and begins to suck out blood through a disk at the head end. Another disk at the other end helps to hold the leech tight while it is sucking.

"Am I going to die?" All children in 1876 had seen death in their own families and around them. Dying happened too often for them not to think of it. A book for young ladies who wanted to nurse the sick said never whisper in the sickroom and especially do not whisper to the doctor, because then the young patient will be sure he is dying. But if he asks the question, the nurse should always keep up his hopes. The proper answer, according to the book, was, "We are all in God's hands and the healthy and strong may even now go before you." There is no record as to how cheerful this news made the young patient.

The hospital was called the "Deadhouse." No one went there voluntarily in 1876, because everyone had known too many people who never came out. Mothers did not even go to the hospital to have their babies. Most doctors thought that if they washed their hands carefully, they would be clean enough to operate. They did not wear surgical masks, gowns, or even gloves, although they did sometimes wear aprons to keep blood from spattering their good suits. There were stories that doctors were not always sure when a patient was dead, so a bell was attached to the toe in questionable cases. If the bell rang, the patient was not dead yet.

Doctors had learned much about anesthetics in the past few years. By 1876 they could operate painlessly, which was certainly an improvement from the patient's point of view. Doctors, though, were still not sure exactly how much anesthetic would put a patient to sleep during an operation and how much would put him to sleep forever.

They knew how to give blood transfusions, too, when a patient lost too much blood. Curiously though, some of these transfusions worked and some did not. No one was sure why.

"It's fate," doctors said, shrugging their shoulders when a little boy died right after a blood transfusion, while another boy immediately began to improve. Both of the transfusions had been given in just the same manner. The same man had given his blood to both boys. What then had gone wrong? It was not really fate. Doctors did not know in 1876 that people have different blood types. A boy with type O blood could not live with type A blood in his veins.

Often the smallest operation killed a patient. No appendicitis operation had ever been successful. Only two years before, a famous British surgeon had said that no surgeon would ever be able to operate on the abdomen, chest, or brain and expect his patient to live. In only a few years he was proved dead wrong.

One of the greatest medical discoveries in history began because France was in debt after the Franco-Prussian War, which ended in 1871. A brilliant French scientist named Louis Pasteur had helped save France's silk industry a short while before. Now the French government called on him for help again. Was there any way he could think of to make French wine ferment more quickly? If so, the sale of wine could get France out of debt.

Pasteur had always thought that fermentation was helped along by living organisms that came from the air. He called them bacteria, or germs. Other people had insisted, though, that the organisms that caused wine to ferment and milk to turn sour had been dead and then suddenly leaped to life by "spontaneous generation." Now was Pasteur's chance to prove that they were wrong and he was right. The wines of France began fermenting on schedule and within three years the debt was paid off. But something far more important had really happened. Pasteur had discovered germs!

After hearing about Pasteur's experiments, a teacher of surgery in Scotland named Joseph Lister started some serious thinking. For ten years now he had been talking about germs to an audience of people who would not listen. Doctors had always thought that the pus around a wound was a normal part of the healing process. Lister knew that during the War Between the States in America, four wounded soldiers had died for every one killed in battle. Why? Just suppose, Lister thought, the pus around their wounds was not fighting the infection, but *was itself an infection* caused by germs? In his hospital in Edinburgh, Lister sprayed everything in sight with

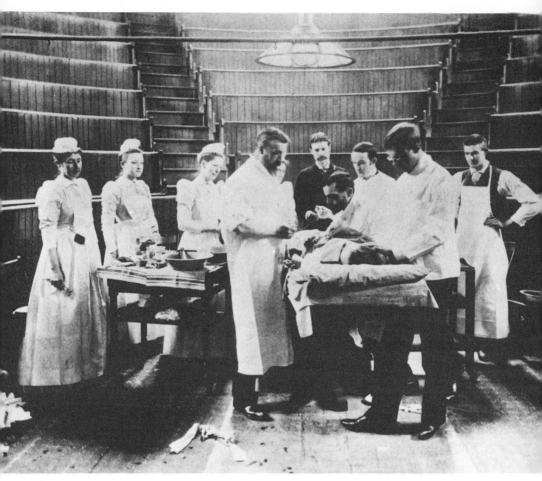

The operating room at Philadelphia's Pennsylvania Hospital—a little later than 1876. Doctors still did not wear surgical gowns, masks, or gloves

carbolic acid—his instruments, his hands, the open wound, the bandages, the whole operating room. His patients healed perfectly —and without any pus in their wounds. Lister was overjoyed with his discovery. But how to tell it to the world? He packed his valise the summer of 1876 and sailed to Philadelphia, where he had been invited to speak before a medical convention during the Centennial. Now he really had something to say!

Lister was not the only man to have news for the world. Robert Koch's wife had bought him a microscope and he was keeping his eye on something suspicious. He thought it was a germ and suspected that it was responsible for a disease known as anthrax. The mystery was that anthrax was a disease in both animals and people—and the people who caught it might never have been near an animal that could have the disease. So how had they caught it? Koch spied on the germ for weeks, watching its whole life cycle. For a while it lived on the hide of a hog. When the hog was killed, Koch found that the germ had not died with the hog as he had expected. It was still living on the dead hog's bristles. Later, when the bristles were made into shaving brushes, he found the germ still very much alive. A man who cut himself shaving could easily catch the disease from that germ. Of course no one listened to Koch, but very soon he and Lister and a few others would have their day.

Meanwhile, diseases and epidemics were being blamed on everything except germs.

"Diphtheria is caused by turning down the wicks of the kerosene lamps too low," said one doctor. "Nonsense," said another, "it comes from drain poison." (He was getting close.) "Consumption" killed more young people than all the other diseases. But what caused it? Was it from not having enough outdoor exercise, or too tight corsets on ladies, or eating the wrong food, or having too small a chest, or too wild dancing, or from "overtaxing the brain with too much book learning"? Actually many children were catching this disease from the milk they were drinking. Some cows had tuberculosis and milk was not yet pasteurized, but Robert Koch did not uncover the tuberculosis germ until six years later.

When there seemed to be nothing else to blame diseases on, there were always "the miasmas." Miasmas, or vapors, were smells that came from nearby swamps, garbage dumps, or sewage. The odor was especially bad when the weather was hot and moist. That was the time when epidemics started—cholera, malaria, and yellow fever (also called "yellowjack"). That was also when the mosquitoes were in full force, but no one noticed that insignificant fact.

"It's the miasmas again," commented the evening newspaper on a hot summer night. "However, as soon as the cold weather comes, the miasmas will be destroyed."

In July of 1876 some people in Cuba caught yellow fever. That was not too unusual for summer. In Texas, border people felt the "yellow fever breeze" stirring. It was a hot wind that came up from Mexico.

"Yellow fever is caused by the oranges and bananas they grow down there," Texas people said. And so no oranges or bananas were allowed over the border while the breeze lasted. People who lived along the border drank whiskey with mustard seed in it to keep from getting the disease.

Then, in August, some people in Georgia came down with yellow fever. By early September, there were four hundred people sick with it in Savannah alone. People began to panic.

"It's the strong northeast wind and rain. They are disturbing to the sick," people said.

A doctor from New York, Octavius White, went to Georgia to try to trace the sickness back to the first victim. At last he traced the disease to a schooner out of New York—a seaman had been taken sick while his ship was tied up in Savannah harbor. But the disease had not appeared in New York—only in Cuba and Georgia. The doctor learned that ships from Cuba had been docked on both sides of the schooner.

Because the nights were hot, the Cuban sailors and the American sailors had slept on the decks of their ships. Then Dr. White checked on victims #2, #3, and #4. They all had been Cubans who had gone to a cheap boardinghouse near the waterfront and had taken with them their mattresses and blankets. There was no doubt in Dr. White's mind that the bedding of the Cuban sailors had brought the yellow fever into Georgia. When he investigated further, he learned that the Cuban ships had used clay for ballast. The old clay had been dumped overboard because the shipload going back to Cuba was heavier and the ballast was no longer needed. That did it! The clay from Cuba must be letting off "mephitic vapors." People began to move as far away from the harbor as they possibly could.

But there was nowhere to go. People could not go back into the lowlands, because there, the doctors said, the porous soil let off "septic miasmas" when the sun beat down on the Georgia swamps. By the middle of September, one third of the city had left town. Two thousand persons were sick. There were so many dead that the supply of coffins had run out. Stores and offices were closed. Soon other cities in the South began counting their sick.

Doctors and health officials were kept busy burning all the clothing and bedding of people who had died. Doctors inspected the ships in the harbor. They changed their clothes before they left the ships and burned those they had worn. Sulphur was burned in rooms where people had died. The chairs and beds were washed and varnished. Georgians did a lot of housecleaning those weeks, but they were not hot on the trail of the villain.

Dr. White began to notice a strange pattern in the disease. It would let up for a while and then get worse. He found that if there were no new cases of yellow fever for two weeks in an area, then no new cases would occur. Sometimes it seemed to be contagious, because persons who were close to each other would all catch it. Other times they did not. Perhaps only certain houses were infected. Sometimes a person visiting a yellow fever patient in the very height of the disease would not catch it himself—or he would get it weeks later. There were too many *whys* for Dr. White.

People continued to drop from yellow fever even though everything possible was being done to keep it from spreading. First they became nauseated, then came the pain in the back, the head, and the limbs. Even before the high fever came, the patient knew what he had. No medicine seemed to work for sure, so everything imaginable was tried. One doctor even invented a kind of air conditioner in the hopes that a cooler room would help bring down the fevers. But nothing worked. "After twelve hours," the folk proverb went, "the victim was either ready for his cook or his coffin."

This is one mystery that was not solved in 1876. Five years later, after he had studied the histories of yellow fever epidemics, Carlos

Finlay of Cuba was able to supply the missing link. Finlay believed that the disease had been carried by mosquitoes. The open barrels of water on the decks of the Cuban ships and the mosquitoes that had come over with them had been the guilty ones. Dr. Finlay was made fun of and laughed at for years—until 1900. Then Dr. Walter Reed was sent from the United States to Cuba to find the cause of yellow fever. He said Dr. Finlay had been right all along.

If doctors had their problems and lack of admirers in 1876, they at least were more popular than dentists. The best invention that ever came to dentists was "laughing gas." Now they all had signs in their windows proclaiming that they did "painless extractions." Most of the patients a dentist saw needed their teeth pulled out because they did not see a dentist until they were desperate and hurting badly. Many dentists could not afford to buy a full set of the delicate tools needed to clean out cavities and fill teeth properly. They did do a large business in making artificial teeth and designing gadgets that held false teeth in a person's mouth—until the wearer sneezed, anyway. Thanks to the Centennial—with exhibits of false teeth from several other countries—artificial teeth were about to get some much-needed improvements.

Many small towns did not even have a dentist. "Dr. Beebe, dentist of Winnebago, will be in town June 1st and remain a week or two. Those having business in dentistry should bear this in mind," said a local newspaper in 1876. Everyone hoped that if he was going to get a terrible toothache, it would arrive while the dentist was in town. If not, Dr. Beebe's place would be taken by another traveling dentist in a week or two. Or three. People with badly timed toothaches had to be satisfied with oil of cloves and chloroform on a piece of cotton stuck into the hole. If the pain got too bad, sometimes they put chloroform on cotton and stuck that piece in the ear nearest the tooth.

A child hardly ever saw a dentist in 1876. Mother removed a loose tooth expertly by tying one end of a piece of string to the tooth and the other to the handle of an open door. When the door was slammed shut, the tooth flew after it—provided the patient stood still. Some home remedies for cavities, though, were so bad that often the rest of a tooth rotted, and the gums became infected.

No one in 1876 knew that infection from the teeth could spread throughout a person's body. That discovery was forty years in the future.

There was no toothpaste. Mother made tooth powder in the kitchen and, as usual, did not even try to make it taste good. A mixture of Peruvian bark, prepared coral, ground chalk, myrrh, and orris root has hardly ever been one of a child's favorite tastes.

"The breath of a well child should smell as sweet as that of a cow," said a medical book in 1876. If a child's breath was not so good as the cow's, he should brush his teeth with finely powdered charcoal in addition to using the tasty tooth powder. Charcoal was black and gritty, but it did make the teeth look white. There were exceptions to using the tooth powder, though. Many people used Castile soap instead to brush their teeth. It was a matter of preference. Every week, the teeth were also supposed to be brushed with plain vinegar to remove the tartar.

Too often sicknesses left behind lifetime reminders. Scarlet fever and other diseases left many children blind or deaf. In a way they were lucky. Sixty years before, there would have been no help for them. But Louis Braille had invented a way of teaching the blind to read through their fingers, and by 1876 there were very good schools for the blind. The deaf children had schools and also a college in Washington, D.C., named for the Gallaudet family, who had pioneered in finding ways for deaf children to learn to communicate. Just four years before, Alexander Graham Bell had introduced a new way to teach deaf children to use their vocal cords. Now he was working on some sort of electrical hearing aid, but so far it had not worked.

Crippled children were not so lucky. No one was working yet on any inventions to help them. There were a great many diseases that left children badly crippled. Soon the housewife who was watching the flies to see whether they were fat or skinny would realize that those same flies could bring such diseases into her house. Soon all houses would be putting screens on their windows. But not yet.

The worst problem that all handicapped children had to face in 1876 was prejudice. There was still a strong feeling that calamities happened to children because God was punishing their parents for something they had done. Many people were ashamed of their handicapped children because of this feeling and kept them hidden inside the house.

"Treatment for the insane is much better than it used to be," said an 1876 newspaper. In the old days, doctors had played tricks on the insane to shock them out of their insanity. One trick was to have the unsuspecting person walk across a room and drop suddenly through a trapdoor into a tub of cold water. That treatment had not worked. Now doctors were experimenting with color. Some rooms had been painted red, blue, or violet. One patient who had not eaten for days suddenly asked for a meal upon entering the red room. A patient in a straitjacket was immediately calmed down on being put into the blue room. And the patient in the violet room asked to go home because he felt all better and "has been well ever since." The colored rooms showed that doctors were at least trying to help people with mental problems.

The world's first psychology laboratory was still in the future. People were trying hard to explain criminals by classifying them into types and doing a very bad job of it. In 1876, most people believed that there was "a criminal type" of person and that that individual would turn into a criminal no matter what his environment or background. There were no intelligence tests yet to tell whether one person had more mental ability than another. There was no occupational therapy in homes for the insane. Only fifteen years before there had been shoe-mending, carpentry, and needlework, but right now caretakers felt that the inmates were incapable of doing anything useful and so they just sat.

Mentally handicapped children had an even worse time than the physically handicapped in facing the rest of the world. Their parents were ashamed of them because they had no idea why their children were not completely "normal." Besides prejudice, there was superstition. In a little community, the townspeople felt that if all the retarded children in the town could be carried off to an institution where they could never be seen again, then the curse of feeblemindedness would never return to their area.

That is what happened to little Martha Nelson, who was four years old. Her parents took her to a home for the feebleminded in

Ohio on June 25, 1875. They had no way of knowing just how retarded little Martha was—only that she was not completely like other children. There were no tests to find out whether Martha could live a useful life outside a home or not. Martha was still living in the home when she passed her 102d birthday in 1973!

The parents of a very bright child were just as worried. An "Advice to Mothers" book warned that children who were too smart had too much arterial blood overdeveloping their brains and they were likely to snap at any moment and go insane. As soon as parents discovered that a child was brighter than ordinary, they were supposed to send him off to a quiet country place, free from the excitement of the town, and put him in the care of a schoolmaster who would promise not to overwork his intellect. Above all, he should not be allowed to compete in anything. Medals and prizes were for children with moderate abilities, not for those with great abilities. It was hoped that if the parents were not too late, the child might be slowed down so he could become like other children.

Altogether 1876 was not too dangerous a year to live in—for people who didn't expect good nutrition from the ordinary diet, take any patent medicines, meet any mad dogs, see any quack doctors, get delivered in a hospital, need a blood transfusion or an operation, live anywhere near mosquitoes or flies, catch any serious diseases, act too smart or too dull-witted, or take off their winter underwear just because the thermometer hit 85° for two days in April.

5

ADVENTURE AND SPORTS

A Bridgeport, Connecticut, man narrowly escaped losing his scalp last week. He had decided to go to the Black Hills, but was taken sick and died two days before he was to start.

—from *Frank Leslie's Illustrated Weekly*, 1876

For boys who found home too dull, there was still some excitement left in the world. For girls who found home too dull, there were many books telling them how best to adjust to the dullness. A boy still had a good chance of becoming a millionaire overnight by discovering a vein of gold.

General Custer's men were patrolling the Black Hills region when they found that the place was full of gold. There was one slight drawback. A great deal of the gold happened to be on land that had been given to the Indians for a reservation. Until word of the discovery got out, the Indians had been complaining about the land given to them. They did not want to be shoved into a small corner of the Dakota Territory. They did not even like the log cabins the Government had built for them to live in.

"Indian live white man's house. Get sick. Die."

Their complaints were not without reason. They were getting sick and dying, but it would be many years before either they or the white men knew that their coughs were caused by consumption, a white man's disease the Indians had never known. But for the time being they used the log cabins to store tools and food given them by the Government. They lived outside in their teepees.

In spite of the Indians' feeling that they had some rights to the gold on their own land, thousands of white men began packing for the latest gold rush. These men had been too young to go to California in 1849. Now they said good-by to their families and caught the next train for Yankton, the capital of the Dakota Territory (now in South Dakota). As usually happens at the edge of gold rush country, the prices in Yankton were way out of bounds. Bacon was 15 cents a pound; sugar, $12.50 for one hundred pounds; wool blankets, up to $5 a pair. Horses were an unbelievable $200, and even then some were completely wild and unbroken.

At Yankton, the eager men heard stories about strikes like the Homestake Mine. George Hearst had bought some property in the Black Hills, although not in Indian territory. He had been making money in mines before, but his wife was complaining about not having a real home.

"George, if you find a good mine," she said, "let's have a home stake." That particular mine of George's—the Indians called him "the boy the earth talks to"—was more than just a good mine. It was the largest gold mine in the western hemisphere—and today, a hundred years later, it is still paying off! Only one story like the discovery of the Homestake Mine would have been enough to start a traffic jam of prairie schooners reaching from Yankton to the Black Hills.

When the seventy-sixers left Yankton, they still had five hundred miles to travel to where the gold was—at about 4 miles per hour (ox power was slower than horse power). They met army troopers who told them that the Indians were giving gold miners a bad time. When the prospectors finally arrived, many of them offered to buy land from the Indians. Others just started looking for gold without giving the Indian owners a second thought—except to keep their guns loaded. The army had its hands full trying to keep down the Indians and keep back the gold-hungry men who thought of an Indian as some kind of animal. Many miners found that it was not easy to run from Indians when their pockets were full of gold ore and lost their lives trying to save it.

There were other areas to explore, such as the Arctic; but so little was known about that region, and the climate there was so vicious that a group of explorers could not be outfitted warmly enough for survival. Thirty years before, Sir John Franklin, a British explorer, had disappeared somewhere up there, and many search parties had tried to find out what had happened to his group. Finally a really scientific exploring party was about to leave for the north to collect data about the unknown frozen country for future explorers.

Getting ready for such a trip at that time was about like getting ready for a launch to the moon today. First there was the problem of what might happen to men living close-packed during 120 days of darkness. What would happen to their minds? Would they go berserk and wander crazily off into the snow? Scientists really did not know. So they did just what NASA scientists were to do with astronauts one hundred years later—they planned every moment of the explorers' days.

"Keep them busy every second" and strictly enforce the rules for exercising, the scientists insisted. There must be very careful sanitary regulations, because even though diseases such as yellow fever and typhoid seemed to be contracted only in warmer climates, this was no time for taking chances and getting sick.

An observatory with no iron parts to cause trouble near the magnetic pole would keep many of the men busy. Astronomical observations were to be taken constantly. Men who were off duty would attend classes in astronomy and navigation.

Choosing the team for the trip was the hardest part. The men had to be skilled—each in a separate occupation. But the men chosen were those who could do more than just their own jobs during those 120 dark days. One man played the banjo, another the flute. There was a drummer and a talented magician in the crew. A piano and a small organ, called a harmonium, were shipped as carefully as were the astronomical instruments. One man planned to teach painting classes, while another would direct plays. A "magic lantern" and a large collection of pictures of "home" went along.

The Arctic was not the only place for the adventuresome. The

Antarctic was a greater challenge—no one knew anything about those southern icy regions. There was no "Little America," and no one had ever found a satisfactory harbor for ships. And there was Africa. Dr. Livingstone's feeling for Africa had made many adventurous boys want to see the "dark continent." Besides, the children of a South African farmer had picked up some "pretty pebbles" a few years back. One of the pebbles was found to be a diamond worth $2,500! A new kind of rush then began.

Meanwhile, there were strange areas in the unexplored western part of the United States. Major John Wesley Powell had just written a book for armchair travelers. He had taken a boat trip down the Colorado River, through the Grand Canyon—and he had something to say. The only men who had traveled anywhere near the same area had sent this official report about the Grand Canyon: "Ours has been the first and will doubtless be the last party of whites to visit this profitless locality." Powell did not agree. When he had read the report of dark canyons with sharp rocky walls, high plunging waterfalls, rapids so swift and deadly that a body falling into them was never seen again, and whirlpools that could pull a boat down into the muddy waters—he could hardly wait to go. After his first wild trip down the river, he went back with a photographer and made many stereoscopic slides that gave people of 1876 their first inkling of what the Grand Canyon was really like.

Dr. Ferdinand V. Hayden carried that project even farther. In 1879 he led an expedition to the Yellowstone area. Hunters had been telling tall tales about that region for years. One of them, Jim Bridger, had said that there were pots of boiling water, a mountain of glass, and water shooting up every so often out of small holes in the ground. It was time someone put a stop to such lies.

But when Dr. Hayden returned to Washington, D.C., he had photographs to prove the stories were true. He made certain that each congressman had some on his desk the very day that Congress was to vote on establishing a national park there. That had been four years before. Other explorers were hoping to talk Congress into creating more national parks—Yellowstone was the only one so far.

Some men who were yearning for adventure found it at hand. Alfred Johnson, a halibut fisherman from Gloucester, Massachusetts, renamed his 20-foot dory *Centennial* and shoved it out into the ocean one day in June, 1876. A week later, he was in Nova Scotia. Then on June 25 he decided to try what no small-boat sailor had ever tried before—at least none who ever lived to tell the tale. He would sail across the Atlantic Ocean in the little *Centennial.*

On August 2, when he was three hundred miles off the coast of Ireland, a terrible storm whipped up the waves. Alfred hurriedly took down his mast and tied it onto his boat so he would not lose it. The little dory broached to in the waves and turned completely over. But Alfred was not a rugged Gloucester fisherman for nothing. Although he had lost everything, he managed to get his little boat turned upright again. Fortunately for him, the rain continued four more days, and he was able to catch drinking water. On August 10, he landed in Wales and was greeted as a hero. The next year when the Gloucester fishing fleet sailed, Alfred was with them—content at last. He had had all the adventure he wanted. But he was called "Centennial Johnson" for the rest of his life.

For some men, just the sports of 1876 were adventure enough. Bicycles were not new. But with the pedal connected to the front wheel, a bicycle's speed was limited by the size of the wheel. The larger the wheel, the faster the bike went. Bicycles had been tossed out by the older generation as being too slow and dull. In 1876 someone had built a bicycle with a really huge front wheel—and there was nothing dull about it.

The main problem was how to ride the thing. Some people never did learn. Obviously this was not to be a sport for women. For the little lady, there was the velocipede. It was heavy and bulky and took tremendous energy just to keep it moving along. Yet in England a few women took bicycle trips beside their husbands— one woman even had a baby on her back.

An instruction book came with the highwheeler. The cyclist was told to get some knickerbockers (pants that buckled tight just below the knees), or at least to tie down his pants legs. The long-distance rider should also line his underpants with chamois or buckskin to ease the wear and tear on the human seat. The first lesson was never to venture out on his cycle without his oilcan (filled with the best sperm oil obtainable) and his spanner (a kind of wrench).

"First, lean the bicycle against a friendly wall," said the instruction book. But the new kind of bicycle had no brakes

Mounting the bicycle was "as easy as mounting a horse," said the book. But the instructions bore no relation to mounting horses. The rider, having learned all about balancing himself by riding a bicycle with small wheels that let his feet touch the ground, now was ready for graduation to the highwheeler. First, he was told to "lean it against a friendly wall." The outside pedal should be at the top and ready to go down. To get on, the rider put his left toe on the step, took three short hops, swung his right foot over and began to roll away from the "friendly wall." He had better remember where that left toe found the step, because he might have to get down again in a hurry. There was nothing to do now but balance and pedal. But no leaning on the handlebars—that unbalances.

Going uphill, the rider leaned forward. Coming down, he leaned way back, put his feet up on a footrest, and prayed. Dismounting suddenly was physically impossible when his feet were stretched out in front on the footrest. After Mark Twain had arisen at 5 A.M. a couple of days to take highwheeler lessons (at an hour when nobody could watch him), he claimed he had invented a whole new book of profane words to go with the sport.

The enthusiast who really took up the sport went on a cycle tour. He might hope to beat the cyclist of the year, David Stanton, in a race. But first he must go in training. That meant getting up at 8 A.M. and eating a hearty breakfast, followed by two hours of complete rest. One game of quoits—no more—was the limit of his exercise until the time was up. Then he could work out on his cycle for a few hours. By then it was time for dinner, followed by another two hours of rest. Then came another couple of hours of work and an exciting supper of oatmeal, and bed before 10:30 P.M. The cyclist knew that he would have a good sleep ahead because the training rules stated that he must never be wakened until his body waked itself.

For the man without a bicycle, there was always pedestrianism. Even women could take part. It was just plain walking. Mark Twain and a friend had been used to taking ten-mile walks. Then they got to feeling very sporty and decided one day to walk the hundred miles from Hartford, Connecticut, to Boston, Massachusetts. After hiking twenty-eight miles, they agreed to forget the whole thing, pledged each other to keep it a secret, and took the train to Boston.

Hunting had meant one thing to pioneers—food. In 1876 hunting was becoming a sport for people who had enough to eat but just enjoyed the challenge. Their guns were not always the best, though the "new" Winchester rifle changed all that.

Meanwhile, many hunters trained falcons to do for them what their inferior guns would not do. A large falcon could be trained to knock wild geese, ducks, rabbits, and other small game unconscious by diving at them with all the force of a bomb. The gyrfalcon, imported from Iceland and Norway, was the superhawk of them all but took about two months to train. Most falconers had to settle for the peregrine falcon—also called a duck hawk—which could be found in New England. This little hawk was easier to train and very graceful.

Trained dogs helped keep the falcon from eating his prey until the hunter arrived on the scene. The first field trials for dogs were held in the United States in 1874. There were only nine starters, but a surprising number of people showed an interest in dogs for hunting. They were all pointers and setters that first year, but by the next year the field trials drew many more people and many new kinds of dogs.

"There would be a power of fun in ice skating—if you could do it with somebody else's muscles," said Mark Twain, who had already proved he was not basically a sportsman. Until the middle of the century, ice skates had been made with wooden or iron blades. The iron was always getting rusty and had to be sharpened right in the middle of a good skate. A man in Philadelphia tried making some skates with steel blades, and the result was a new sport. A few cities even built indoor rinks, called "glaciariums." But most skaters had to find a frozen-over pond to have their fun.

One day an American ballet master was watching people skate aimlessly around in circles—although one was making figure eights—and he wondered why music could not be added. Skating would be much more fun if people could dance on skates. The new steel blades had made figure skating possible. The ballet master started schools to teach the art of dancing on skates, and another new sport began.

At last there was something fun that girls could do—or, as *The Young Lady's Book* said, "for those who have the courage to try to learn it." Skates were easy to put on—they just buckled at the ankles and around the toes. However, the young lady was not exactly up and off across the ice like a flash, because the instructions said that she should skate around with a chair in front of her for balance. A new invention, the sleeve life preserver, had been suggested for people who skated on thin ice. The sleeves were made of cork and were so unbendable that the skater's arms were held almost straight out at her sides. Evidently she did not wear the life preserver until she had finished skating around with a chair! But if the ice broke and she had on her preserver, she would stay afloat until someone could pull her out.

There were other winter sports to keep the cold days lively. Ice hockey had just become a sport at McGill University in Canada, but it would be several years before the Americans tried it. Iceboating started right after the War Between the States. The first ski club had just been formed in New Hampshire. Skis were not new. They had been brought over by Scandinavian immigrants. The gold miners of 1849 had often needed skis. One mailman, "Snowshoe Thomson" had used both snowshoes and skis to deliver mail for

At last—a sport girls could try if only they "have the courage to try to learn it"

twenty years in the Rockies. But skiing as a "sport" was a new idea. No one thought then of ski lifts or tows. The uphill walk was thought necessary to keep a man warm enough for the trip downhill.

No boy with a hammer, nails, and a packing crate was without a sled in the winter snow. Most sleds were the flat kind for "belly-flopping," but steering was hard on shoes. The front bars did not steer—that was done by dragging a foot and throwing the weight around. No matter how good the sledder was, a boy or girl could not go around a corner on the sled. The child might go around it, but the sled would go straight downhill.

Winter clothing was not really made for playing in the snow. Woolen underwear did not have air spaces to keep in the heat of the body as does today's ski underwear. Waterproof pants were good only for a few hours at best. Woolen mittens, the only coverings for hands, had snow clinging to them in chunks and were wet before one hour had gone by. Arctics were boots to help keep the feet warm, but often they needed cork or felt inside them for extra protection. The winter just before 1876 had been one of the worst on record. Great chunks of ice froze at the base of Niagara Falls, and people visiting them had fun sliding down the ice blocks.

During the cold weather there were many new indoor sports, too. An inventor had just improved the wheels of "parlor skates" and now a new roller skating rink had been built in New York City that cost $100,000. Polo, an exciting new sport brought over from India and played on horses, was very new—but at first people thought it should be played indoors. It was much more popular when they got the game outside on a field. There was bowling indoors, too. But in 1876, a bowling alley was the hangout of the worst people in town. Bowling had begun as "ninepins" and had turned into a gambling game. Its reputation was so bad that many cities passed laws to keep its citizens from "bowling at ninepins." That was their mistake. Soon a new game was worked out—bowling with ten pins—and it was more popular than ever.

When the ice finally melted in the spring, and children were allowed to take off some of the clothes that had swaddled them in the winter, most boys headed for a fishing hole. Many girls liked fishing, too, but they knew that it was not a sport for girls because it included wriggling worms and slimy fish on hooks. The girls tried to content themselves with the new game, archery, which was supposed to develop nice chests. Some of them went riding, but there was a lot of discomfort in bobbing sidesaddle, in a ladylike way. Western women were lucky. They could ride "Indian style," straddling their ponies in a manner that would have shocked Easterners off their seats.

Golf had started in Scotland and was just getting to England. A new kind of ball made of gutta-percha, called a "gutty," went much farther than the old balls made of feathers wrapped in leather. Golf was starting to look as if it might be interesting. Golf clubs—the clubhouses—were popular in the United States long before the sport became so.

Colleges put sports on their spring and fall calendars for good in the year 1876. The Intercollegiate Association of Amateur Athletes of America was formed so that fourteen colleges could have rules governing their competition in track and in rowing. An amateur had to be a person who was not paid for using his muscles. This meant that even though he might be the best runner in America, if he had been paid for digging canal ditches, he could not compete. In other words, these were to be sports for "gentlemen" only—no laborers allowed! Amateurs were not allowed to benefit financially at all from the sport they played in—even if they wanted to bet a friend 25 cents that they would win. The rules were very strict. A lawn tennis player was not even permitted to play tennis with a professional or he could not be called an amateur again. Actually the word "amateur" was hardly used in 1876. Instead of "amateur," the word "gentleman" was used to distinguish him from the pro. In horse racing there was the "gentleman rider" and the "jockey"— the professional.

"A game of baseball was played on the cricket field last Wednesday by the Chelsea Centennial Nine and the Franklins. The Franklins won 17–5. The pitcher claims that the ball was slippery, which may account for his not pitching so effectively." It was spring and almost every local newspaper reported the sporting news as in the above notice. No one would have dreamed, in 1876, that

One year after this 1875 picture, the National League was formed and the catcher was advised to wear a chest protector, a catching glove (although it had no padding in it), and a "birdcage" over his face

someday a full page or two might be devoted to sports.

Baseball was forty years old in 1876, but it was a little different from today's game. The umpire tried so hard to be fair in making his decisions that the game stalled for long periods while he took testimony from all the players and all the nearby spectators before declaring a player to be out. And the catcher was often knocked cold because he used his chest as a ball stopper without wearing any protector. He stopped a lot of balls (and bats) with his face too. That was why someone invented a mask, called a "birdcage," modeled after the mask used in fencing. And the batter had a few advantages then too. He could call to the pitcher for a high or a low ball. He also had nine balls before walking to first base instead of four as today. The pitcher stood only thirty-five feet away from the batter, and the balls may have been a little faster coming at him. When one of the pitchers had thrown a ball that curved on its way to the batter, some scientists had said it was impossible. It had to be an optical illusion. But in 1870, Fred Goldsmith from New Haven, Connecticut, proved that he could really throw a curve by doing it eight times.

In 1875 catchers were finally given gloves to help them catch, but there was no padding in the glove to ease the sting of a hard one. The Cincinnati Red Stockings were almost laughed off the field when they had first appeared in short—knickerbocker—pants eight years before, but by 1876 most ball teams wore the same uniform. Teams could choose any color of uniform they wanted.

The National League was formed in 1876. Until then, professional baseball players had belonged to another organization called the National Association of Professional Baseball Players, but that group folded. It cost a club $100 to join the National League, and no city with fewer than seventy-five thousand inhabitants need apply. The clubs that joined were Boston, Hartford, New York Mutuals, Philadelphia Athletics, Cincinnati, Louisville, Chicago, and St. Louis. Immediately the National League set up some standards. The very next year four Louisville players were drummed out of baseball forever for "throwing a game" for some gamblers who did not want to lose their money by betting on the wrong team.

The first National League game was on April 2 when Boston beat

Philadelphia, 6–5. On May 23, Joe Borden pitched the first no-hitter game. But Joe's fame was short—he was reduced to club grounds-keeper by the end of the season. Chicago won the first pennant with 52 wins and 14 losses.

On the first warm day of summer, fathers unpacked the family croquet set. Croquet was really a backyard sport for adults, but many families kept a smaller set for the children to use. As with most sports in 1876, a woman did not have so good a chance to win as a man. It would have been unthinkable for a lady to stand over the ball and swing her wooden mallet between her legs. Because she wore long skirts that reached the ground, a lady was supposed to swing the mallet with an outside stroke—nowhere near so devastating as the wallop a man standing with his feet apart could give. Croquet was so popular that, in addition to selling sets priced from $4.50 to $25, a toy manufacturer named Milton Bradley designed a small, easily packed "tourist" set for people to take on vacations.

Warm days meant boating, too. The wealthy had their America's Cup Race. In 1876, the challenger was the Canadian yacht *Countess of Dufferin*. She lost the race quickly to the American yacht *Madeleine* and the America's Cup remained where it had been since 1851. For poorer folk, there were canoe clubs forming along all the rivers and bays of the country. Rowboats were safer and therefore were recommended for the ladies. The costume for rowing was a long flannel skirt with no crinoline under it and no tightly laced corset. Of course, some doctors said that rowing was too violent for women, but there were some daredevil females who tried it anyway.

In one New York park there was a model-boat basin where children lucky enough to own model yachts could enter a sailing competition just as their fathers did, sailing on Long Island Sound. A prize was offered for the winner by a famous toymaker—a perfect miniature clipper ship with all its parts working. The newspaper stated, "If a boy wins, he can sail the yacht. If a girl, maybe she has a brother or a little boyfriend who can help her."

Poor people did not have time to play games, and there were not many they could enjoy anyway.

Two new sports were just becoming popular with the wealthy set.

Most doctors said rowing was too violent for women. It was a man's sport

One was tennis, though it was not really new, since it had been played on lawns for years. What was new was the tennis court built by two wealthy Bostonians that summer of 1876. The other game had been taken to England from India by several army officers who said it was called "Poona." The name got lost, but the game was popular. The Duke of Beaufort gave a party at his country home, "Badminton," just to introduce the new game. For years it was called "that game at Badminton," until the name was shortened.

"Going bathing" did not necessarily mean going swimming. It meant just what it said. Most people did not swim, even when they went to the seashore. Jumping up and down in the waves was about all women could do anyway in their complicated bathing dresses. But a few cities, especially those on rivers like New York City, really made an honest try at getting their poor people to smell better by providing "bathhouses" by the water. Bathing was so popular that six new baths opened in New York City, along the riverfronts, in 1876.

Ladies' Day at the free swimming bath in New York's East River. Note the ship masts in the background

Admission was usually free. Monday, Wednesday, and Friday were ladies' days. Of course men and women could not bathe together, even though they were as fully clothed as they were when on the street. The bathers took their suits and changed in the dressing rooms. They also took soap and towels, unless they planned to spend 5 cents to rent them. Each bather was allowed to stay twenty minutes and no longer. Even though children resorted to all sorts of tricks to get into the pool a second time, they were usually caught. Once a day was the limit. In the evenings, bathers were allowed only ten minutes when there was too large a crowd. Workers could swim until nine at night so that most of them had a chance to clean off. Every day the pools were scrubbed. The East River baths were more popular in New York City because the river on the west side was always muddy—the water used was straight from the river.

Very few people knew how to swim at all, but it was becoming a sport that people wanted to learn. The previous August, Captain Matthew Webb in England had swum the English Channel for the first time. He had used the breaststroke. Now everyone wanted to learn this wonderful way of staying afloat. The Australian crawl was not invented until much later.

For timid swimmers there was always the dashing Captain Paul Boyton for an example. At twenty-six, Captain Boyton had already rescued over seventy persons from drowning. Then he had invented a "life-saving suit" that he thought should be in everyone's closet—at least there should be one on board every ship. He did not mention which *person* of the sinking ship's company would be chosen to wear the lifesaving outfit.

The suit was made of vulcanized rubber filled with air chambers, making it as floatable as a boat. Each of the air chambers had its tube, so the swimmer could just blow in a little more air to float whichever side of him was sinking. He lay flat on his back in the water, with inflatable pillows under his neck that kept his head afloat, and with a small mast and sail attached to his feet so he could sail with the wind. That wasn't all. The complete outfit included a small raft he towed behind him with his "equipment." The equipment included provisions for ten days, a flagstaff and flags, a

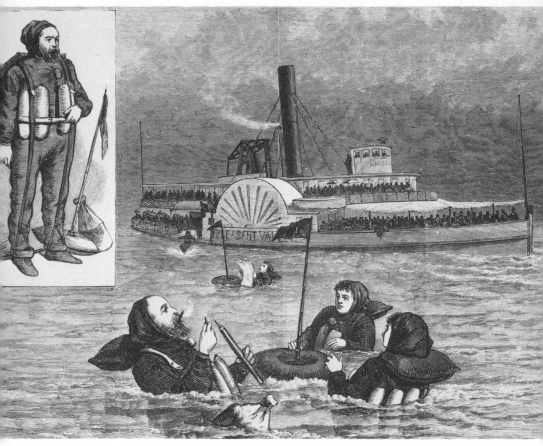

A steamboat filled with sightseers came up the river to watch the brave people testing an 1876 lifesaving suit

small lamp (to see in the dark?), a compass, a foghorn, a revolver (to shoot at sharks?), a knife, a flask, books, signal lights, a small anchor, an ax, a lead line (to see how deep it was), a ship's log, and a thermometer. In addition, the survivor carried a double paddle and a bugle attached to his waist. The paddle was for moving himself along in calm water, and the bugle was to call for help. Actually, Boyton did not use it for that, but to play tunes as he drifted down rivers in the East to show off his invention.

In late October of 1874, Boyton actually jumped into the sea from a steamship that was thirty miles off the coast of Ireland. He picked a terrible time to try out his suit, because very shortly a heavy gale struck. Fifty-six vessels were wrecked that night. After nine hours in the waves, Captain Boyton landed unharmed on the coast.

Prizefighting meant using bare knuckles—there were no such things as boxing gloves. The Marquis of Queensberry had drawn up some new rules that were first used in London in 1872. Said these new rules: no more bare fists—fighters had to use gloves; boxers should be classified according to weight, because it was not fair for lightweights to be fighting heavyweights; also a round should be limited to three minutes instead of being extended until one of the contestants was knocked cold. Besides all this, the match was to be held with the fighters standing up. There was to be no more pummeling the man who was down. The new rules spoiled all the fun, according to many Americans who preferred not to pay any attention to them. The Queensberry rules were not adopted in the United States for another twenty years.

In September of 1876, an American, Tom Allen, was calling himself the champion of the world. Joe Goss of England challenged him and the fight was held in Covington, Kentucky, on September 7. Finally Allen fouled so often he was disqualified in the twenty-seventh round, but he still called himself the world champion. Twenty years later, when John L. Sullivan was the heavyweight champion of the world (with bare knuckles), he suggested using gloves under the new rules.

Rules were getting in the way every time a team of men wanted to play football, too. In November of 1869, Princeton and Rutgers had played an exciting game of "football" in which the ball could be moved only by the foot. With twenty-five men on each side, it was hard to tell where the ball was at all. The gentlemen from Harvard were not too impressed. They organized their own football club in 1872 and played a game with McGill University of Montreal. The McGill team liked more of a rugby type of game. By McGill rules, a player could pick up the ball at any time and run with it. Since there was no oval-shaped ball yet, keeping the round ball in the crook of the arm was no easy job—but the game was more exciting. One by one the other colleges had to agree that the "Boston game" was better. There were only fifteen men on each side. Then, when the game was played in 1874, four of the McGill men did not show up and the teams played with eleven men on each side. The result was that the four men from McGill lost their places on the team, because the game had been better with eleven-man teams.

The game between Harvard and Yale, which Harvard won 4–0, on November 13, 1875, was such a good one that the following year all the colleges met to set up permanent rules for the game of football—adopting many of the rugby rules. The Intercollegiate Football Association grew out of this meeting.

In 1876 a new sport was just over the horizon. Everyone was waiting impatiently to hear more about the Keely motor. One day there was a powerful explosion in the inventor's workshop. Keely, who had said that a teacupful of water could create enough power to drive a train, was having trouble with his engine.

He was not the only inventor with the problem. But others were trying something new. An American, George B. Brayton, had built an engine that used gasoline instead of steam. In January of 1876, Joshua Rose and A. R. Shattuck had a license from Brayton to use his engine and try to build a road vehicle. They had hoped to show their auto-mobile at the Centennial along with Brayton's engine, but their vehicle did not move. The competition was getting fiercer.

An "automobile car" run by compressed air was tried out in France. There was no danger of fire or explosion, said its inventors—at least not while it was moving. The trouble was that it did not move very well. In Germany two very successful men had invented a two-cycle engine and a four-cycle engine. In 1876, Otto Langen and August Otto applied for U.S. patents. One of their associates, Gottlieb Daimler, and another German, Karl Benz, were also close to success with their gasoline motors. In that year it was hard to tell just who was going to win this race. Meanwhile, a thirteen-year-old boy in Michigan was fascinated by all this talk of engines that would move road vehicles. Henry Ford would soon be out of grammar school and wanted to work in a machine shop more than anything.

There had been no Olympic Games since A.D. 392. In fact, the old Olympic stadium in Greece had been wrecked by an earthquake and a few hundred years later was buried by a landslide. But an interesting thing was happening in 1876. Some German archaeologists had begun to dig at the site, and the first part of the old stadium was exposed to light. Within two years, the excavation was complete and began working its magic on people. Talk of reviving the glory of the old Olympic Games began, but it would be another twenty years before talk grew into action.

6

GIRLS WILL BE GIRLS

One hundred years hence what a change will be made
In politics, morals, religion and trade,
In statesmen who wrangle or ride on the fence,
These things will be altered a hundred years hence.

—From a feminist song in 1876

To start with, 1876 was a leap year. That should have been a warning of what was to come. Leap year was always a time when women could be bolder than usual.

The women of Norfolk, Virginia, began their social season with a Leap Year Sociable. Ladies had never dared invite men to a party, but that is what the invitation said. So they invited the men, but allowed the men to call for them and take them home. After all, there was a limit to just how bold a lady could be.

As soon as the couples arrived at the ballroom, the men found out what the leap year might hold for them. The ladies took the men's cloaks to the coatroom. Then they offered the men their arms to go on the dance floor. Their dance programs were filled in by the ladies—a man found that he had his first dance with Susan, the second with Mary, and so on through the evening. He was allowed only the first dance, the last dance, and the one before dinner with the lady who had brought him. Men who had not been assigned a dance partner for a dance had to sit with the other "wallflowers" and wait until a lady asked them to dance. It was the custom for ladies who did not have a partner for a particular dance to line up against a plain white wall that would show them off to good advantage in the hopes that a man would find them attractive enough to ask for a dance. Now the men learned how it felt to be a wallflower.

All evening the ladies took care of their escorts in the very same way the men had always taken care of them. They carried their refreshments to the gentlemen and asked the proper questions: "Are you sitting in a draft? May I get your shawl? Are your poor feet aching?" The men loved the attention they were getting. By this time they should have been growing suspicious. But they were not. After all, this was just a sociable evening. Or was it?

There was something special in the air that night—just as there would be every day of the new year. A rebellion had started just before the War Between the States, but it had had to be postponed during the fighting. Now it was starting up again. This time the rebels would be louder and bolder.

"The movement is becoming embarrassingly militant," moaned one man. Almost every male in the country agreed with him. "Women are just not behaving like women any more!" said Mark Twain, who could usually find something funny to say about any subject. "Now is the time for all good men to tremble for their country."

Women had had it—up to the tops of their starched high-buttoned collars. They were tired of being laughed at as if they were all as stupid as Mrs. Partington. Mrs. Partington jokes were all the rage and each one was based on the idea that women were none too bright. When a woman friend mentions how tall her husband is, Mrs. Partington exclaims, "Six feet in his stockings! Why Ike has only two in his and I can never keep 'em darned at that!"

Women were fed up with being told that their place was in the home, taking care of the children. They had been told so often that certain problems could be handled only by the brain of a man that they were beginning to believe it. Mrs. Stevens joined the rebellion one morning after teaching Sunday school. The children had been real problems that day and she decided to talk it over with her minister. She did not want to be a quitter, but perhaps he could help. Here is what she wrote in her diary that night: "My work in the Sunday School is exceedingly difficult. Dr. Starkey says it requires a male mind to present these truths with clearness. If he is right, then I may retire from the field with a good conscience." Next morning, Dr. Starkey was out trying to recruit another new Sunday school teacher and wondering why he had to ask so many women before he found one.

Women who had brains were told that they could not use them. Women who had talent to paint were supposed to paint flowers, not pictures with emotional content. When a male art critic first saw the paintings of Mary Cassatt, his only comment was, "I refuse to believe any woman can paint like that!" Women writers often hid behind men's names in order to sell their books. Emily Dickinson had written some poetry that was years ahead of her time. She filed away in her bottom bureau drawer all her poetic thoughts—lines such as, "I'm nobody! Who are you? Are you nobody, too?" This was the year that women were going to declare their rights.

But just how was a girl going to revolt when she was wearing a corset so tight she could hardly speak above a whisper? How could she march for freedom when her shoe soles measured only two inches across and her feet were all of three or four inches wide? How could she show men she was not weak when her dress hugged her knees so she could not take a normal step and her collar grasped her throat so tightly that she could not lower her chin enough to look at her feet? The revolution would have to begin in a clothes closet.

Girls' clothes made no sense. Boys could wear knickers that were loose at their knees. They could bend down easily to play marbles or scramble under a bush. When they climbed trees or stretched up to catch a ball, their shirts pulled out. But a tomboy girl trying the same exercise soon found her dress torn at the waist and her sleeve ripped out at the shoulder.

When little boys went home filthy dirty, their mothers sighed, and their fathers said, "Boys will be boys." They had tough materials like homespuns and blue jeans that stood up to hard wear.

STYLES OF GARMENTS;

FALL, 1876.

~❧ LADIES' PATTERNS. ❧~

4506 **4506** **4504** **4504** **3958** **3958**

Ladies' Half-Fitting House Dress: 13 sizes.
Bust measures, 28 to 46 inches.
Any size, 50 cents, or 2s. Sterling.

Ladies' Princess Dress: 13 sizes.
Bust measures, 28 to 46 inches.
Any size, 50 cents, or 2s. Sterling.

Ladies' French House-Dress: 13 sizes.
Bust measures, 28 to 46 inches.
Any size, 35 cents, or 1s. 3d. Sterling.

3751 **3751** **4188** **4188** **3820** **3820**

Ladies' Gabrielle House-Dress: 13 sizes.
Bust measures, 28 to 46 inches.
Any size, 35 cents, or 1s. 3d. Sterling

Ladies' Evening Dress: 13 sizes.
Bust measures, 28 to 46 inches.
Any size, 50 cents, or 1s. 9d. Sterling.

Ladies' Plain Princess Robe: 13 sizes.
Bust measures, 28 to 46 inches.
Any size, 25 cents, or 1s. Sterling.

3311 **3311** **4350** **4350** **4324** **4324**

Ladies' 'Metropolitan' Riding Habit: 13 sizes
Bust measures, 28 to 46 inches.
Any size, $1.00, or 4s. Sterling.

Ladies' Box-Plaited Wrapper: 13 sizes.
Bust measures, 28 to 46 inches.
Any size, 40 cents, or 1s. 8d. Sterling.

Ladies' Wrapper, with *Tablier* Front: 13 sizes.
Bust measures, 28 to 46 inches.
Any size, 40 cents, or 1s. 8d. Sterling.

Ladies were hampered in their fight for freedom by their clothes. Note the riding habit in the lower left corner

Not even their best trousers had a crease down the front, because no trouser material then made would hold a crease after a few hours' wear.

Girls' knees were just about useless for things like creeping under hedges or boosting them over walls. They were covered by long white stockings, even on hot summer days. Dresses always hung down below their knees even when girls were very young. And when they came home with torn aprons and battered stockings, no one ever said, "Girls will be girls." They had to learn how to be ladies very early and to squelch all those unrefined wishes to be free like boys.

When a girl was twelve, she could start wearing a corset. At least, the fashion designers said she could. From this year on, she would be a battleground for dress designers and doctors to fight over. Doctors blamed everything from consumption to crooked backs on girls lacing themselves up too early. They said wearing dresses with padded busts kept a girl from developing the way nature intended her to. Bustles made a girl's dress heavy and caused a strain on her back. High boots stopped the circulation in her legs. So did garters. She should hold her stockings up with supporters that hung from her shoulders. After a few years of battling, the girl usually won out over the doctor. She did not want to be "unstylish" even if it did mean all those dreadful things the doctors said. So she squeezed herself into the current popular shape, tripped along with dainty steps, and tried to learn a new way of breathing.

As in every teen-ager generation, there were a few strange fads for girls in 1876. One was wearing enormous buckles that "looked like shiny pie pans in their wide belts." Another was having holes bored in their ears for earrings. And then there was the "lunatic fringe." That was the effect made by brushing the hair over the forehead so that it hung down in the eyes.

Most of the elegant dresses came from Paris. There a designer named Charles Worth tried to tell women that they should dress according to their own individual taste. Having a "Worth gown" was the ultimate in fashion. Later, when Mr. Worth died, Mark Twain joked that dresses from Paris were now "Worthless," but American women did not agree. Each lady wanted a fancier dress

"What the well-dressed lady will wear to the Centennial," according to Peterson's Magazine, *looks hot, uncomfortable, and heavy*

than her friends had, and she was willing to spend a great deal of her father's or husband's money to get her wish.

"These dresses are cheap in everything but the price," one father groaned. The basic dress was fairly reasonable. It was all the "extras" to go on it that cost so much—braid, beading, ribbons, feathers, lace, and buttons. One father was so angry at his daughter's clothing bill that he took her newest dress apart and measured how much ribbon was on it—he found 4,320 inches.

A lady needed a special dress for each occasion. A man could wear "country clothes" (there was no such thing yet as "sports clothes") for many occasions, but a woman could not. The etiquette book for the year devotes thirty pages just to telling a girl what dress to wear when. A morning dress, for instance, could be made of cheap material, but it was unthinkable to wear outdoors a dress that cost less than 25 cents a yard. (Multiply that by twenty-five yards of material needed for just the skirt and remember that the average worker earned about $10 a week.) A girl needed a dress to go calling in and a different one to receive callers at her house. She needed a church dress (but could not wear the same one every Sunday!), a silk dress for formal occasions, a black dress for mourning (always someone was dying), a walking dress with a long skirt for indoor walking and one with a shorter skirt for walking on dusty sidewalks. She could not wear a horseback-riding dress to play croquet, or to ice skate, or to go to the theater, or to walk at the seashore. The father of an active teen-age girl was buried in dressmaker bills!

If it had not been for the sewing machine, which could by 1876 be in every home, and for Ebenezer Butterick, the poorhouse might have been filled with fathers. One day when Mrs. Butterick was trying to make a dress for her child, she mentioned how much easier her job would be if she had a pattern. That had been thirteen years before. In 1876, the Butterick Company published a fashion magazine and sold thousands of patterns every month. Almost any woman could sew her own clothes with these.

"Great," said the men. "Sewing their own clothes will take their minds off this ridiculous feminist movement." But they were wrong. The women had more time and more reason. Now they could make their own clothes a little more comfortable.

The clothing that went underneath a dress took as long to put on as the dress. A girl wore a shirt and bloomers and a short wool petticoat under her long one if it was very cold weather. Some dresses had a "dust ruffle" that hung slightly longer than the dress in the hopes of catching most of the dirt from the floor or the street. Supporters hung from the shoulders with long tabs to attach to the tops of long stockings. Stockings were sometimes very fancy, with embroidery on the sides. They were very rarely silk—usually lisle or cotton. A younger girl's stockings showed because she did not yet wear dresses to the floor.

Then came the important part—the bustle. Bustles changed every other year. In 1876 a framework of coiled wire helped a girl support the extra weight of her skirt. The bustle itself was a pad filled with cotton or wool. The dress material was draped elegantly over the top. Some dresses needed the "dress improver." It helped to gather the dress material and bunch it over the hips as well as over the bustle.

Only country girls were still wearing tunics. The new thing was the basque. A French princess had gone on a fishing trip in the Basque country of France. The weather had suddenly turned cold and the princess had slipped into a Basque fisherman's jersey sweater. Being very fashion-minded, she fastened her belt over the top of the sweater to make it fit snugly—and began a new style. In 1876 every girl wanted a basque bodice, or "waist," that went down below her waistline and flared out over her hips.

The dolman sacque was new too. Ada, who lived in the country and never had a dress that wasn't handed down, thought her friend Libbie had everything a girl could want. "Libbie was dressed splendidly," Ada confided to her diary. "She wore a lovely dark blue suit trimmed with black satin folds. She had a sack [Ada did not know any French spelling] and overshirt [a basque waist] of course."

A girl could not ever be sure that her feet would not hurt. By 1876 machines were pouring out ready-made shoes, so that there were hardly any shoemakers left who knew how to fit a foot. Many pairs of shoes did not even have a proper right and left foot. Soles of "indoor" shoes were very thin, but even for "outdoor shoes," linings of felt or cork had to be added for warmth in winter. This did not help the way the shoes fit. Liquid rubber was painted on the outside of outdoor shoes to help make them more waterproof. For very bad weather, there were india-rubber boots, or arctics.

Indoor shoes for girls had pointed toes. Outdoor walking shoes had square toes and were more roomy, but a girl could not just slip her feet into them and walk away. Kid boots had buttons from bottom to top—about fifteen on each foot. The only way to get them buttoned fast was to use a buttonhook, which was a part of every lady's dressing table set. The wearer put the small hook through the buttonhole, grasped the slippery button with it, then carefully pulled the buttonhook back through the hole. If she was skillful, the button came through the hole too.

The most popular shoe with young girls was the "Reine Margot." It was made of kidskin, soft as a handkerchief and just about as wearable. It had a single strap with a metal buckle instead of a button, because buttoned dance slippers were too childish for a young girl. Heels were getting higher and they were no help to a girl who was trying to support a bustle while already standing like an S.

Most girls and women did not carry handbags. Instead, a girl had a pocket hidden among the folds of her dress to hold a "reticule" (also called a "ridicule"). One teen-age girl dropped her reticule on a street in Nebraska. It was found by a man who took it to the local newspaper office to advertise for its owner. Since there was no name inside, the newspaper listed the contents instead:

> Two white cotton handkerchiefs with hems bigger than the balance, candy fish, 1 short slate pencil (black and chewed at the end—too hard at the other), 1 bit of blue ribbon, 2 bits in money, 1 piece short black scalloped ribbon, one elastic garter without buckle, 2 short pieces barber pole candy (1 peppermint, 1 lemon), a pair small black kid gloves, 1 parasol tassel, camel's hair brush, 1 love letter (very tender, praising her and running down another girl), 1 horsehair ring (unfinished), 3 hair pins, 1 perfume bottle stopper, 1 box of breath perfume, a ball of floss, a broken crochet needle, a small piece of raw cotton full of white powder, the left heel of a #2 gaiter, 1 stocking with a hole in toe, a thimble, and a nutcracker. The pocket is of yellow nankeen and can be obtained on application at this office.

Although the new bathing dresses for young people were quite revealing (exposing ankles, arms, and throats), swimming in them was next to impossible

---

The rebellion of women actually might have begun at the seashore. Nowhere else was the inequality of men and women so very evident. A boy wore a two-piece bathing suit, with his arms and legs bare. The sun could shine on his neck and face. He could even swim if he had to.

A girl did not have a chance. She wore a long dress that hung well below her knees. Under that, she wore long pants down to her ankles or else thick stockings. Very young girls could wear short sleeves, but a young lady over twelve covered her arms to keep them from tanning. Her dress was fastened right up to her throat or "men might look at her." She wore a hat with a wide brim that was tied on securely to shade her face.

But rebellion was only a few thousand miles away. Word came back from the West that women on the Pacific Coast had refused to wear the traditional striped stockings for bathing. They were wearing flesh-colored ones instead! A thousand miles in the other direction, some French women had been seen bathing in the Mediterranean with no stockings on at all! The newspapers of the New Jersey shore resorts notified its readers that any women as bold as those would be arrested on the spot.

Mrs. Amelia Bloomer thought women should wear a sensible "national costume." The one she suggested had a short jacket and short skirt worn over long pants, which came to be known as "bloomers." They looked a little like the Turkish costumes at the Centennial. The idea was a little too strange for most women and very much too strange for men's liking.

In Philadelphia, a group called the Free Dress League tried to petition Congress to appoint a committee to consider what sort of dress would be suitable for the women of this country to wear. This group made men angrier than ever. "That just goes to show you," they raged, "the sort of thing that female influence is likely to bring into our politics if women should ever be allowed to vote!"

In Boston, the National Dress Association, founded by women, sent out speakers. It was easy now to reach an audience of women because women's clubs were being formed everywhere. Each small town had its lyceum, or small lecture hall, where "educational" talks could be heard. In the country, the Granges held meetings for women. The ladies spread the word among themselves, and the audiences grew.

In Ohio, Sudie Evans went to a lecture and wrote a letter to her cousin about it:

"Mrs. Susan Everitt lectured about what the ladies should wear and eat to keep well and young. Hundreds of her admirers are crazy about bran bread without butter. No tea or coffee or meat, but a little broiled beef or mutton once a week without pepper or salt. She told them they might fill up with beans and potatoes with the skins on and eat them without salt, skins and all. That would make them so smart as there is so much electricity in the skins. . . . She would burn 6 bushels of coal a day that cold spell we had and have 4 windows open in her room at the hotel. . . . She went strong against medicine which she says is killing more than wars, famine and pestilence."

Without the help of telephones, radios, or television, every woman in town soon heard that something was going on down at the lecture hall. In another letter, Sudie Evans says, "Miss Anna Dickinson began her course here on Woman's Rights. Mrs. William Lindsay attends all of these. She was here today telling me about it. I was much pleased with what she said. And I believe I shall go hear her. Fifty cents a night seems too much, but the people attend by the hundreds . . ." And so another convert was added to the list.

Now that the women were listening, it was time to move away from the topics of clothing and change something else that had been keeping the ladies' rebellion from getting started. Many of the old ideas had to be turned off. The ladies themselves had been encouraging the very attitudes that were keeping them helpless.

First there was that old notion that "a *lady* was weak and dependent." That was humbug said the speakers for women's rights. Women could be just as strong as men if they wanted to be. Mothers had been raising their children to be healthy—but not too healthy. Pale skin was considered much more refined than rosy cheeks and tan skins. Many mothers of the upper classes would have been ashamed to have a daughter who was as strong as an ox.

"Those pioneer Western women are a different breed," Mrs. Newton said to her friends when they called for afternoon tea. "My Julia is too delicate for that kind of life."

Julia's family was very rich. Her father had died when she was fourteen. Her mother and sister enjoyed their life of tea parties, trips to Europe, and calling on friends every day. But not Julia. Often she spent whole days in bed. She liked to paint, draw, and write stories—when she "felt strong enough." She absolutely hated driving in the country. The most strenuous game she ever played was croquet. The servants worried about "poor Miss Julia." Down in the kitchen they talked about how a person could die from having nothing to do. Eventually Julia would get up and put on her dressing gown until after the noon meal. Sometimes she played the piano, but mostly she wrote in her diary.

From all sides, Julia kept hearing that she was "not very strong" and must "save her strength." Yet no doctor could ever find anything wrong with her. One year her mother decided Julia should go to Egypt with them. Everyone who was *Anyone* went to Egypt "for their health" that year. Julia met many interesting people and had plenty of energy to enjoy every dance the entire winter. Egypt was fashionable in the winter, but Rome was the place to go for Easter. So Julia, her mother, and her sister packed their trunks again and headed for a stylish hotel in Rome. In less than two weeks, Julia had caught typhoid fever and was dead—a tragedy that could happen to the healthiest. But to Julia's mother it was proof that her daughter really was delicate.

The feminists were determined to change people's thinking about women being weak. They pointed out as an example Mrs. Custer, who rode alongside her husband and lived a life of great hardship, yet she behaved like a lady.

The next idea that had to be changed was that a lady had to be dependent. Many women thought that "having to go to work" was about the worst calamity that could happen to a well-brought-up girl. To make sure that this never happened to their daughters, many parents saw to it that their girls never learned how to do the kind of work a girl was paid for. It was all right for a girl to learn how to bake a cake, but only a servant girl learned how to bake bread.

Kate Coffin was a girl who had been raised to think that way. Her father had been a bodyguard of General Washington, and had been a wealthy owner of a shoe factory. Kate would never have to earn a living. Her husband would care for her after her father was gone. But her father died before Kate got married, and after a few years, Kate ran out of money. She had been raised to believe that a woman should be supported, and since there was no husband, there was only the poorhouse left. So she moved into an almshouse and there she lived, being "supported" as a lady should—for thirty-seven years.

Another dangerous idea that women had heard since childhood was that "a girl's growing brain will not bear much book learning." Many people really believed that a girl who had too much education would lose her mind. Not only that, they thought that no man would want to marry an educated girl.

Within the last few years before 1876, high schools were free and girls were allowed to attend. But talking their parents into letting them go was the hard part. What a waste it was to educate a girl who would only get married and raise children anyway! A girl who was really far out and wanted to go to college had an even worse time. After she finished convincing her parents that she should go, she had to find a college. She usually had to go to one of the women's colleges because not many universities or other colleges accepted girls in 1876.

Tragedies did happen and sometimes a girl did have to go out to work. If she had no education, there was hardly anything at all she could do. Even the girl who had been to high school and learned shorthand and bookkeeping was going to have a very hard time in the business world. Everyone worked from ten to twelve hours a day and every day except Sunday. There was no such thing as the "weekend," because Saturday was a workday just like all the other days. Even if men and women had not wanted to work such long hours, there was no such thing as a union to help them change the minds of their bosses.

Employers liked to hire women because they did not have to be paid nearly so much as men to do the same jobs. The male superintendent of one post office in 1876 earned $3,000 a year. The pay for a female superintendent was $825. The mail clerk earned $2,000. A woman got $550 for doing the same work.

The working conditions were terrible, and this is one area where women's rights groups went to battle. One large industry that hired thousands of women was the garment industry. Making "ready-to-wear" clothing was a new industry since the War Between the States, and factories were filled with women sewing pieces of clothing together. They spent long hard hours (never dreaming of a coffee break) bent over their sewing machines. The lights were poor gaslights or flickering kerosene lanterns that gave off bad, gassy smells. The rooms were too hot in summer because there were no electric fans yet and too cold in winter because the factory owner was not about to pay for heating the building any more than he had to.

Another of the women's battlegrounds was at the saloons. Thanks to all the medicine that was full of alcohol, the country was filled with alcoholics. They were not called alcoholics then, because no one knew yet that alcoholism is an illness. They were just called "drunks" and put in jail if they got out of hand. The money their wives and children needed was spent on liquor in a corner saloon. One wife who had tried to reform her drunken husband was Carry Amelia Moore. Her husband was a doctor. When he died, Carry was so furious at saloons and liquor that she could hardly control her temper. In 1877, she married again and with her new name, Carry Nation, later became famous across the country as the woman who carried a hatchet and really destroyed saloons.

But in 1876, before Carry Nation got started, the saloons were scenes of a more peaceful type of destruction. Large groups of women paraded down to the corner bars and knelt to pray and sing hymns in front of the doors. Even the worst drunk found it hard to enjoy his whiskey with the ladies outside. The Woman's Christian Temperance Union managed to close many saloons and breweries with their tactics. Unfortunately, the alcoholics needed more help than a closed saloon could give them.

The most important battle that ladies fought that year, however, was against the laws of the country. Suffragists were trying to do much more than just "get the vote" for women. Susan B. Anthony said, "Women want bread—not the ballot!" Already there were some states where women could vote. The liberation leaders felt that if women could vote in all states, then they might have a better chance to get some laws passed that could help them.

The ladies expected the men to oppose them—and they were not mistaken. Almost every man in the country seemed to be on the other side. Mark Twain said that if women voted, all the smart ones would vote like their smart husbands and all the dumb ones would vote like their dumb husbands. And the results would be exactly the same when the votes were counted, except that each candidate would receive just twice as many votes as before.

All the laws in 1876 were on the men's side. A woman had hardly any rights at all. Her father was her boss until she was married. Then, at the wedding ceremony, he "gave her away" to her husband, who took over. She really belonged to him. Everything she once owned was now his. He could spend her money as he pleased, choose her friends for her, separate her from her relatives, change her religion, and he had the right to beat her if he wished.

A mother did not even have control over her own children. If her husband wanted his children to be raised by a family down the street, he could give them away. Children belonged to their father. He could demand that they work for him and put them in jail if they did not obey him. Many teen-agers in 1876 were sent to reform schools and industrial farms by their fathers to "turn them into good children." The children, and that included all under eighteen, were given no trials because they had no rights either. Even a child who stole bread might be sent to an adult prison. Juvenile courts were more than twenty years in the future.

Legally a wife did not exist without her husband. He could not give her any property except through a trustee. Only since 1872 had she been allowed to keep any money she earned herself after marriage—and only with the court's permission. And the court would not permit it if the husband objected! No husband left everything to his wife when he died. If there were children, she could have one third of the property. If she had no children, she could not have more than half his property—even though the property might all have belonged to her family before she married him.

A wife could do no business unless her husband joined her in signing the contracts. There was one exception. She was allowed to contract to buy a sewing machine and pay for it on time payments. This was the only way a poor widow could earn a living—sewing clothes and paying for her machine at the same time. A wife could not be a corporate member of any institution—even though she may have given it a great deal of money. The only exception to this rule was an institution run by women for the care of children, or for the sick and indigent.

Lillie Jordan discovered the power of the law when she danced with a gentleman friend at a Centennial Tea Party in February 1876. Lillie had known Curtis for many years, but it was not until after she had married another man that she realized Curtis was the man she really loved. "Too bad," her husband and friends told her. "You're married now." Lillie only wanted to dance with Curtis, but her husband commanded her not to. So did her brother-in-law and her own father. The other guests at the dance must have enjoyed watching the commotion.

Lillie was high-spirited and perhaps something of a liberationist. She danced with Curtis anyway. The next day Lillie's baby, little Francis, was taken away to live with his grandparents until Lillie was "brought to her senses." Lillie went home to her father, furious. She tried once to kidnap her son, but failed when the grandparents got suspicious. They kept the baby. Lillie's husband told her that his "wounded pride" could only be soothed when she admitted she had done wrong and regretted her sinful act of dancing with Curtis against his commands. Within a year, Lillie had gotten a divorce— one of the very few given that year and a great scandal to both families. She was married soon afterward to Curtis. But baby Francis belonged to his father, and Lillie never held him again.

There were plenty of rebellious women in 1876 who had the courage to do the jobs they felt needed doing. Every jail, poorhouse, and lunatic asylum keeper knew that the knock he heard at his door might turn out to be Dorothea Dix, demanding better conditions for his inmates. Clara Barton had just seen the horrors of the Franco-Prussian War and the brave group of men who had saved many lives on the battlefield after the fighting. In 1877 she began a campaign to establish the Red Cross in the United States. A lady lawyer, Belva Ann Bennett Lockwood, was in Washington trying to have a law passed that would allow female lawyers to argue before the Supreme Court. A deeply religious woman, Sojourner Truth, was working that year to improve living conditions for Negroes who had freedom but no comfort. Harriet Tubman, who had helped more than three hundred slaves to escape during the war, was working to start schools for Negroes in North Carolina. Emma V. Brown, a graduate of Oberlin College, had opened the first "colored public school" and was principal of another school for black children.

In 1876 some of the young people were starting out on lives that would not follow the traditional rules for young ladies. Annie Oakley at sixteen could already outshoot any man in her territory. Jane Addams had decided to be a doctor at sixteen, but within the next year her friends at Rockford College, Illinois, would help her realize that social settlement work, not medicine, was to be her goal. Another sixteen-year-old, Juliette Low, was one girl who could never understand why girls could not have as much fun as boys. Someday she would organize the Girl Scouts of America.

The rebellion for women still had a long way to go. The year 1876 was only one year—even though it was a day longer than some years. But there was a change in the air. "One hundred years hence" there really would be many changes.

7

TAKING A TRIP

Ho! for cheap trunks so strong and nice
We are selling now at any price
And traveling bags both fine and neat
At prices that cannot be beat.

—From an 1876 advertisement

Trunks in 1876 had to be tough enough to ride through rain and sleet strapped onto the roof of a stagecoach or to hold their own with cargoes of cattle and lumber in a railroad freight car. One traveler was so angry about having his trunk always squashed underneath other trunks that he invented the "Saratoga" trunk. It had a rounded lid so that no other trunks would stay on top of it. But one of the worst trips a trunk had to take was to be unloaded from a ship.

"The sailors made a sort of sliding gangway from a long piece of canvas," wrote one ship traveler. "It stretched from the steamship deck down to the deck of a little tugboat. All the trunks slid, rolled, and jumped down, and landed in a jumbled mass on the deck. Many were broken and forced open. No regard was given to the protests of the owners."

Americans were good travelers. Most of them had had to travel to get to this country in the first place. But now something entirely different was happening. People were starting to take trips just for the sake of taking a trip. For the first time, they had a little extra time for something called a "vacation." A few could afford to take trips just out of curiosity to see a little of the world beyond the small area they lived in, but most trips were very short.

"Uncle Harry took us for a drive on the pike. We had a great time taking down the bars—no less than eight times."

Taking a ride on Uncle Harry's "wheels" may not sound like a trip exciting enough to write about in a diary today. But for Mary Elizabeth Jonas, her sister, and two brothers, it was a big event.

Mary Elizabeth's family lived in a large city and they could not afford a carriage of their own. Only once had their father rented a carriage from the livery stable and that had been for their grandfather's funeral. But every time Uncle Harry came to town, he took the children riding. On those days, Mary Elizabeth undid her pigtails and let her hair fly loose in the wind as Prince trotted faster and faster through the city streets. She did wish that she were allowed to ride up front as her brothers did, but she sat meekly with her little sister on the bouncy black leather seat cushions.

"To the pike, Uncle Harry!" the children demanded.

Some of the back roads were bumpy, especially when Prince started going very fast. Often there was room for only one carriage at a time, and Uncle Harry had to pull over to let another pass. But the pike was smooth and was two lanes wide near the city. Drivers had to pay to use the pike. After Uncle Harry paid, the bar across the road was taken down and a whole new section of the pike was opened up to the explorers.

"We took Prince and the carriage and drove down the river road about three miles," Mary Elizabeth wrote at the end of another hot summer's day. "On our way home we bought some ice and when we came home, Mama made lemonade!" Another bonus of "fast" travel on the pike was that they could get home before the ice melted.

When a father went to a carriage shop to buy the family's transportation, he had to decide first whether he wanted two wheels or four. Two-wheelers were faster and more sporty. They were perfect for a young man to take his girl out, but they were not much use for taking the family. Four-wheelers had better springs, too.

Springs could make a lot of difference in the way a body ached at the end of a trip. A family that lived in the country hardly ever rode on a smooth road. The smoothest ride was in the ruts, but the ruts were not always the right distance apart for every set of carriage wheels.

Before he decided on the carriage, the father had to think of his horsepower too. One horse could pull a two-wheeler, but a buggy with four wheels needed two horses. Horses had to have a stable, plenty of food, and a person to take care of them.

A sporty one-horse runabout was made of a resilient kind of wood to help add springiness for bouncing over potholes and ruts. The wheels had dish spokes to help get through the mud, which might often be two feet deep. Although most wheels were flat when laid down, dish-spoked wheels were curved like a dish. Some runabouts had only one seat with a box under it to keep baggage in. Such a runabout was a popular buggy for a country doctor. But there were no brakes on it. If it broke loose from the horse, it was advisable to aim for a grassy or any soft spot and jump. Another small runabout was a gig. One person alone could not drive the gig, though, because it would not balance unless there were two people in it.

The most practical carriage was a wagon that could be converted to passenger use by adding removable seats. It also had a top that could be put on in bad weather. There were drop curtains at the sides to keep the rain from pouring in. The driver, however, got thoroughly soaked because he had to sit outside.

A brand-new kind of carriage was the tallyho coach. It had been copied from the English coach used to deliver the mail. But it was brought over to the United States about 1876 for sport. A man who owned a tallyho belonged to a select coaching club and when he went driving, he was a sight to see. His four horses wore plumes and had been trained to step just so. Their harness gleamed in the afternoon sun. The driver dressed elegantly in special clothing and carried himself proudly. Sometimes he announced his coming with a flourish on a bugle. Tallyhos were not for just anybody.

The tandem hitch—attaching one horse in front of the other— was much harder to manage than two horses trotting side by side. Only certain types of rigs were hitched tandem, because if the

These passengers on the California–Oregon Stage Line were in for a bumpy, and often dangerous, ride

horses were not handled skillfully, they could easily upset the carriage.

The new carriage buyer had very little choice of color. He could buy black. A few wagons were yellow, but they were not for family use. In Paris, where people were not afraid to be different, a man could buy a black carriage with a blue stripe or even a dark-blue carriage with one red stripe and one green one.

Most families who could afford a carriage chose a black phaeton. It had two seats facing forward and was not too hard to drive. A pair of horses could pull it. Some were even designed low and were easy to get in and out of so they could be driven by a woman. One, called a basket phaeton, was light enough for one horse—provided the passengers were not too fat.

Four-in-hand driving is the kind seen in most Western movies. Four horses pull a Concord stagecoach with one driver handling all four horses, even though Indians or robbers were closing in fast from behind. Concord coaches were still being used long after 1900 in parts of the country where no automobiles or railroad tracks had yet reached.

Concord coaches were rugged, but the ride they gave the passengers was anything but comfortable. Their main feature was that they usually got the passengers where they were going in more or less good shape. Weather curtains kept out the rain and possibly even a few Indian arrows. Inside, the passengers held on to strong leather straps to keep upright when the going got rough. A folding seat between the two facing seats could be used for extra passengers or to brace the feet against.

No one needed a driver's license. Even children could drive their small runabouts on the roads. There were few good roads. A turnpike was not necessarily a good piece of road. Sometimes it was made as a shortcut or as a better road than the existing one. Sometimes it was the only road. There were no road maps. Drivers of coaches always knew the best roads and the best taverns to stop in for meals or for a change of horses. For long trips, fresh horses were needed about every six hours if the driver was to keep on a fast schedule.

A livery stable rented carriages for special occasions. Frank was a nineteen-year-old schoolteacher in a small village. He earned $16 a month. On that pay he could hardly afford a girl friend, much less think of marriage. But he was in love with Kate and one day he talked a friend into renting a carriage so they could take their girls blackberry-picking on a nearby mountain. But the friend backed out of sharing the expenses.

"My girl's father won't let her go," his friend sulked.

Frank counted the money in his pocket again and decided to rent a two-wheeled buggy. He climbed into the seat and took the reins. He felt like a millionaire behind the snorting little brown horse. Kate was impressed beyond words when she saw him drive his sporty runabout up to her house and leap out to help her into the seat.

But when they were halfway up the mountain, the rim of one of the wheels broke. While Kate stayed with the horse and buggy, Frank walked back with the broken wheel to find a blacksmith. He had to waken one by pounding on his door. With much fuming and sweat, the blacksmith finally managed to bind another iron strip around the wheel's rim. Frank started back up the mountain road rolling the wheel before him. It was noon before the wheel was safely attached and the pair again started up the rocky mountain road.

Within a few hours they were happily picking blackberries. The horse, still attached to the buggy, followed them through the fields as well as it could. But before they noticed, the shadows grew longer.

"Shouldn't we be starting back down?" Kate asked suddenly.

They had worked their way over to the western side of the mountain, forgetting how much darker it would be on the eastern side, where the road went down. By the time they had driven over to where the road should be, Frank could not even see any space between the trees where he thought the road emerged from the woods onto the field. He had not even thought to bring a lantern, and there was none with the buggy, since it had been rented for a daytime ride only. For two black hours, they rode slowly around the field trying to find the road. Kate began to cry. Frank comforted her as well as he could, considering his own feelings. It wasn't just the cost of a horse and buggy for another day that worried him. It was fast becoming obvious that they would have to spend the night on the mountain. In 1876 that meant Frank must do the gentlemanly thing—he asked Kate to marry him.

As soon as the sun was up, they gathered more berries for their breakfast. The horse had been loosed from the buggy for the night.

"The horse is gone!"

Frank and Kate searched all morning and part of the afternoon. Finally, with aching feet and hearts, they gave up and started down the mountain, slipping and sliding on the stones. They met a man with a wagon who took them to a farmhouse. There Frank managed to rent another horse so he could take Kate home. Then he rode back up with the farmer's horse to bring down the buggy. But Frank's run of bad luck was not quite over. The carriage pole broke and had to be mended. At long last, Frank got the carriage back to the livery stable. The next day he took off on foot and succeeded in finding the missing horse. By the time the man at the livery stable had been paid off, Frank had $3 left in his coat pocket. He used it to buy a marriage license the next day.

"Summer tramps" was the name for people who took a vacation in the summer. It was a brand-new idea. Unfortunately the traveling conveniences that we take for granted did not exist then. There were country inns, but no one could be sure of having a room entirely to himself. Innkeepers had a code—they never refused a traveler just because there was no room. They simply woke up a man who was happily sleeping in a double bed and told him to move over for another traveler.

Also, the traveler could not just point to a spot on the map and say, "I'm going there tomorrow," because sometimes there was no way to get from one place to another. The summer of 1876, Mr. Jordan, from Philadelphia, took his wife and two teen-age daughters to the White Mountains in New Hampshire. Today that trip would require about two days in a station wagon, using four-lane highways most of the way.

The Jordans' trip began with a sea voyage to Boston.

"We had a very pleasant voyage," reports Mr. Jordan in his diary. Then he adds cheerfully, "Everyone was quite sick on the steamer."

His wife, Emilie, and two daughters collapsed in a Boston hotel room, trying to forget the sea part of the trip and concentrate on the rest of the vacation that Mr. Jordan had told them would be such fun.

They took a train to Lake Winnipesaukee. Trains were quite comfortable providing that the passengers only opened the windows when the wind was blowing the soot from the locomotive away from the train. The trunks were loaded into a baggage car and the ladies into the parlor car. Each lady had a seat of her own that swung around to face the windows or to face the inside of the car. Mr. Jordan spent most of his time walking through the cars, talking to the conductors and brakemen, and resetting his watch as the time changed. He had carefully chosen a train equipped with the new Westinghouse vacuum brakes (later called air brakes) so his family would be safe. They reached the lake just before bedtime.

Next morning he had to herd his family, and their trunks, onto the boat dock to catch the lake steamer. His daughters were not looking forward to getting on a boat again. Happily, this ride was calmer. After another night's rest, the family and the trunks were loaded onto a stagecoach for a forty-mile ride into the mountains. They were more than ready for a rest after that ride. Each day there was a thirty- to forty-mile stagecoach ride. Finally they arrived at Mt. Washington. Even though there was a full gale blowing and sleet that nearly froze them, the Jordan family made it to the top of the mountain, pulled in a wagon by six strong horses.

The Jordans saw enough sights to last them a lifetime. Each day they packed their trunks and themselves into another stagecoach, rode about thirty-five miles to the next hotel, and collapsed into bed again. The girls had a great time riding on the top of the coach every day that it did not rain. By the time they reached home, they had traveled 1,500 miles. In all their trip, they never knew what it was like to have springs under their cushions or foam-rubber padding. They never had a hot bath or a cool swim in a swimming pool at their tavern stops.

The railroads had opened new worlds to people who could afford only short trips. On the twentieth of June, Sarah Doran went to the seashore with her grandmother. In the old days it would have taken

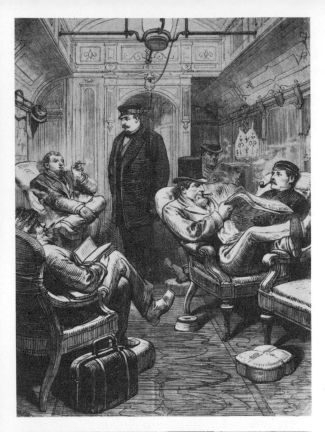

The gentlemen's smoking saloon on a train included a neat, round cuspidor for men who spat.

Chairs in the new parlor car made passengers as comfortable as their own parlors

all day to drive a horse and buggy from Philadelphia to Cape May, New Jersey. In 1876 it took less than two hours each way! The train ride was hot, but none of the forty people sitting on the board seats cared. Soon they would be feeling the cooling ocean breezes. Only the vendors in the train were a nuisance. They would drop oranges and sandwiches in people's laps or shout loudly to attract attention to the newspapers or lozenges they were selling.

But all discomforts were quickly forgotten when the train arrived at the station and the crowd moved toward the public bathhouses to change into their bathing costumes. Not even a very young girl could tear off her stockings and dash into the water to wet her feet. That would have been very shocking. While Sarah put on her bathing dress, Grandmother kept telling her how things used to be. "When I was a girl, ladies could swim only when the lady's flag was up on the pole. It always seemed to me the men's flag was flying just when I wanted to swim most."

Sarah had heard Grandmother's story before. Eventually so many women drowned that the town authorities thought it was safer to allow men and women to swim at the same times. Thank goodness she lived in a modern age, Sarah thought, as she struggled into her bathing outfit. Finally she set her straw hat on her head, tied it on tight, and was ready . . . almost. There were still her india-rubber bathing shoes to put on. They scrunched when the water filled them, and sometimes the sand washed in, making them too tight for her to walk without limping. Sarah envied the boys greatly. They could allow their faces to get tanned. She knew her friends would make fun of her if she allowed her skin to tan. Only very poor people who had to work all day in the hot sun got brown in summer.

Sarah had no idea how to swim. She only jumped up and down in the waves. She knew that if she got out too deep or if a strong wave pulled her out to sea, she would be in bad trouble because her dress was very heavy when it was wet. For this reason, she carried a cord around her belt. She never knew exactly how she was supposed to throw the cord when drowning or when being carried out to sea on a wave, but she guessed that she would do the right thing if the time ever came. Grandmother had read in a book that the surf would lubricate her joints like oil, and Sarah supposed that would help in case she began to drown. She waded only waist deep.

The same book—Grandmother kept it on the bookshelf at home—also said that no child should swim in the ocean more than a half hour—and even that was to be during the morning. One doctor even said five minutes was long enough for any child. Sarah was glad he was not her doctor. She thought it was hard enough to leave the enticing ocean when Grandmother told her the half hour was over. When she was younger, she had begged to go back into the water for just one more dip. But she knew better now. There was a brisk half hour of walking after swimming, then it was time to put on street clothes again.

Afternoons at the seashore were for getting dressed up. The only people who swam during the afternoon were the maids and people who did not know any better. Children dressed in their best clothes and followed their parents up and down the boardwalk until time for dinner. They could wear sunglasses that made everything look blue and carry a parasol if they did not have a sun hat. Children who were lucky enough to spend the night at the seashore could look forward to an evening walk or perhaps a music concert and early to bed. Breakfast had to be finished two hours before the morning swim. Sarah and her grandmother took the afternoon train back to the city because Grandmother did not trust the chilly evening air.

People who had never traveled anywhere in their lives were thinking seriously about it that summer of 1876—because of the Centennial Exhibition to be held in Philadelphia. Every magazine and newspaper was packed with stories about the remarkable things to be seen at the fair. Special cheap excursion rates to the Centennial city were being offered by all the railroads. Many large businesses gave their employees a Centennial holiday. But many country people had never been on a train and had never stayed in a hotel. The newspapers tried to answer all their questions in advance.

"Telegraph or write for a room reservation," began the article on "How to Stay in a City Hotel" that appeared in every small-town newspaper in the United States in May. Most rooms would cost about $5 a day, but rooms could be found in guesthouses for as little as $1 a day. Hotel guests were told that each hotel would have a public parlor for the use of all their guests. In the dining room the headwaiter would assign a seat to each person. The guest would eat each of his four meals in that seat—the extra meal was tea. There would be special tables where children and their nursemaids could eat away from the grown-ups.

The railroads advertised too, because many country people were afraid to travel on trains. Before the new air brake, there had been too many accidents, but with its use, the railroads said, accidents were almost impossible. The railroads even told people much more than they wanted to know. For instance, the steel rails weighed 67 pounds per yard of rail. And there were 2,600 oak railroad ties in every mile of track.

"Going in the cars," as people called railroad travel, was more luxurious than ever by 1876. Some trains had sleeping cars in which the chairs used by day could be turned into beds at night. Heavy curtains gave each compartment privacy. The dining cars were no longer located at the side of the tracks, except in the West. In some trains the passengers could eat in a dining car attached to the train. The seats in parlor cars were velvety, with adjustable backs. And best of all, the trains traveled at a constant speed of 40 miles an hour.

The hardest part of traveling on a train was finding out what time the train arrived and departed. Standard time had not been invented yet. Until fast-moving trains had begun to bring the faraway cities closer together, there had never been any reason to standardize time. There was clock time and there was sun time. Sun time changed every day as the days grew longer or shorter. So clock time was the "right time," meaning that when it was noon in New York City, it was 55 minutes and 25 seconds after 11 A.M. in Philadelphia. And it was 47 minutes and 53 seconds after 11 A.M. in Washington, D.C. That made it exactly 11:30 A.M. in Cleveland, Ohio, but in Albany, New York, it was already one minute and six seconds past noon! Trainmen became famous for their ability to tell passengers exactly what time it was at the very spot in the country where they asked the time.

If there was ever any doubt that the railroads were the travel of

"Waitin' fer the train to go by" was a popular entertainment at small-town railroad stations

the future, the Transcontinental Express set people straight. Two theater producers dreamed up the idea of having a train travel straight across the country without stopping. Even they did not believe it could happen, but it did! Five railroad companies cleared their tracks, and on the first of June, 1876, a Thursday, the train left New York. It was filled with people who had paid $500 each for a round-trip ticket. The catch was that this train was going only one way. The passengers had to come home via ordinary train.

The Transcontinental Express had a baggage car, a day coach, and one Pullman car. The Pullman included a kitchen and an icehouse so that the cook could provide meals without having to stop. Twenty-one hours after leaving New York, the train was passing through Chicago. At every railroad crossing there were bonfires as people all across the United States joined in celebrating the event. Even in the smallest town everyone was down at the railroad station to watch the Express whiz by. Across the plains, the train sometimes went as fast as 50 and 60 miles an hour, which explains why people out that way called it the "lightning train."

But nature was not cooperating. Rains near Ogden, Utah, washed out some of the track, and a telegram had to be sent back to the speeding train saying to slow down in case the track could not be replaced in time. But the workmen from Ogden did not want to stand in the way of progress. They worked all night to fix the damage. Just in time, they laid down their tools and cheered the lightning train as it flew past. The train arrived in San Francisco at 9:39 A.M. on Sunday, June 4. The elated passengers, who had helped to make history, hurried to the nearest hotel to take baths and then to start making arrangements for the slow, painful ride back home.

The Centennial city was not the only place to which people were traveling in 1876. Wealthy people had always gone to Europe to "take the waters" at a spa where hot, bubbling, and smelly mineral water came up out of the ground. That year the not-so-wealthy were discovering that the United States had many spas too. "Taking the waters" meant not only drinking some of it but bathing in it as well. Everything from corns to cancer was supposed to be cured by doing one or the other. Some of the medicinal springs trickled out of the ground. Some spouted up in geysers of hot water. Usually the water tasted horrible and therefore was supposed to be very good for a person. Going to a spa was the thing to do, socially, in 1876.

Traveling on land was certainly much safer than traveling at sea that year. Although ships were built strong and moved fast, a captain still had only his "sea sense" to tell him where he was in a fog or storm. There were no lighted signal buoys even in New York harbor. There were some lighthouses that could be seen fifteen miles offshore in good weather. And there were lightships anchored in bad spots where a lighthouse could not be built. But in a bad fog or storm nothing could be seen of their lights until it was too late. A new type of signal buoy was being tested. It had a horn on top that made a noise as the buoy danced in the waves and was called a blower.

There were no ship-to-shore radio signals, no bell buoys, no Coast Guard. Telegraph operators sent their best guess as to the coming weather, and this information was given to captains before they left port. Once the ship had sailed, there was no way to let a captain know he was heading straight into a hurricane.

All types of ships were sailing on the seas. Square-riggers made the long trips. There were many sleek new steamers, but they still carried masts because sailors could not trust the engines yet. Clippers were the fastest ships built, but they could capsize if they heeled over too much. They were considered great for passengers, but a horror for their crews. Swift new sailing cutters and schooners made short trips up and down the coast. Some very slow, lumbering old tubs made trips up and down the coastline, too.

Chester and Ben were farm boys in Maine. More than anything in the world those two wanted to see the big Centennial. One day Ben suddenly got an idea of a way to do it. Ships were sailing from Maine to Philadelphia all the time. All that the boys had to do was sign on one and work their way.

"That's a crazy idea," said Chester.

They sailed the twelfth of May, and Ben began his diary of their trip: "Here I am in the forecastle which is to be my home for the next four weeks. It is about seven feet square, containing four bunks which resemble my mother's sink as much as anything I know of."

Before the trip even began, the two boys had sore hands from hauling on the ropes and sore backs from loading blocks of granite into the hold. The night before they sailed, they both "went up to the village to see the fashions"—meaning the girls. They also snitched a lobster from a lobsterman's trap and had the ship's cook fix it for their supper. They were mighty sorry the next day. About midnight their schooner was towed out of the cove where they had loaded her, and they anchored in the river until a breeze came up that would carry them out to sea. They had been on the waves just a few hours before Ben began to feel strange. "Cuss the sea!" he wrote in his diary. "Wish I had stayed home. Sick as the Old Harry. Tried to eat something at dinner time, but was obliged to part with it when I went up to the mast head to grease it. The rolling of the vessel up there made me worse."

The heavy ship rolled miserably. The wind blew from the wrong direction, so that it seemed as if they were getting nowhere at all. The next day Ben gathered enough strength to write in his journal again. "Still alive. *Never* want to hear anything more said about the grandure of the ocean. It is all a humbug. I hate the sea and I guess the sea hates me. Haven't ate anything since yesterday at dinner. Don't feel as though I should want anything more to eat *ever*. If you get tired of home ever, go to sea. And my word for it, you will come back content and happy even if you live in a log shanty."

That afternoon the captain's wife took pity on Ben—or maybe her husband was just needing his new deckhand upright instead of flat on his back. She took him some oatmeal gruel and talked him into keeping it down. At suppertime he went down to "take a look at the victuals for fear I might forget how they looked and ate a little." That night he was able to go on watch "to see we do not run into any vessels."

A thick fog came up and the captain had to turn back to the nearest harbor. Ben's seasickness was forgotten. He was scared now instead.

"We got out an emense fog horn which was handed to me with the inquiry if I was musician enough to blow it. I had to blow 3 blasts, then pause, then repeat it again. The ocean was very rough. The steward said the largest waves he'd seen in a year. . . . Some would rise 18 feet, then break and roll in on the deck. When the vessel was down in the trough of the sea, they would rise and appear to be coming right over the vessel. Then she would rise to the top of them. Then take another plunge down. One wave came over the bow and completely drenched us. But didn't I just enjoy it! At anchor now. I will turn in as the bedbugs must be getting impatient for their supper."

Chester and Ben made it to the fair. No ship was ever unloaded faster as they sped to finish their chores so they could see the sights they had come for. The sea voyage—and the return trip to come—were soon forgotten as they took in the fair.

On the way home the boys discovered that the captain had a streak of meanness in him. Since on his ship, as on most small coastwise ships, the captain had to pay for the meals out of his own pocket, he gave orders for the ship to ride uncomfortably—just during the meal hours.

"Same old fare for grub," Ben's journal complains. "Beef and bread for breakfast and bread and beef for dinner. Guess I can stand it for a week or so longer anyhow. I have seen the Centennial and that is glory enough for me."

The designers of the new steamer *The Bessemer* were thinking of travelers like Ben. This ship had a specially built saloon called the "floating cabin." The entire room could move like a gyroscope. When the ship tilted, the floating cabin was straight and therefore no one could get seasick in it. But after thousands of dollars were spent to build it, the cabin was renamed "the cabin that didn't work." It was for sale in 1876.

The newest thing in shipping was to be called the *Frigorifique*. This "refrigerator ship" was being built in France and would soon carry foods on a grand scale. It would sail with luxuries such as wine, cheese, butter, and fresh vegetables to South America. Then it would carry back to France fresh meat, game, fruit, animal skins, silkworms, and eggs.

For years Edwin Greble had been reading the advertisements of steamship companies. On the American Line, he could sail to Liverpool, England, for $75 to $100, first class. In 1876 it was becoming clear that steamships would soon replace sailing ships. He would go on one of the newest steamships, Edwin decided. But he was realistic enough to know that even steamships were not perfect yet.

"I had made up my mind to take all things philosophically," he wrote in his journal the first day of his trip. "Otherwise I would be apt to encounter much trouble and vexation."

He was so right. People who felt any other way in 1876 were better off staying at home. The moment Mr. Greble walked up to his cabin he knew that he would have to struggle to be philosophical

A traveler could cross the Atlantic in ten days on the sleek new steamship Ohio. *It carried masts, too—in case the boilers did not work*

———•◆•———

enough. The room he was to share with another man was the size of one queen-size bed. Already the other man's baggage filled all the floor space. They would have to dress lying down in their bunks. And he had selected one of the "large" staterooms from the plan shown to him at the shipping office!

The *Scotia*, a steamship that also carried masts and sails, left the harbor in a dense fog with its steam whistle blowing every five minutes all night. Next morning Mr. Greble found one of the reasons why people liked steamships. It was bitterly cold and the smokestack was completely surrounded by passengers who were trying to get warm by leaning on it. People who had been lucky enough to receive a basket of fruit for their sailing presents were munching apples and pears because the "acid" fruits were supposed to keep a person from being seasick.

It took eleven days to cross the Atlantic by steamship. Even when the ship did reach the other side, no one could be sure of getting off where he had planned. On this trip there was a terrible storm, and the steamship had sent up rockets to let the pilot boats in Ireland know it had arrived. Several passengers had planned to get off there, but the seas were so rough that the pilot boats could not come near enough to take them off. So they had to sail on to England.

Another kind of schooner was sailing across the prairies in 1876. Prairie schooners were not so graceful as the old Conestoga wagons that the first pioneers had used, but they had more space inside. Since they tipped upward at either end as had the Conestoga wagons, the furniture and other baggage inside did not slide around so easily. Their main feature was their huge white canvas top that gave them the appearance of ships sailing on the prairie.

The traffic going through Yankton in the Dakota Territory during the summer of 1876 was as bad as in any present-day city during the rush hour. One of the groups traveling through was the party of General and Mrs. Custer. Elizabeth Custer had been traveling most of her married life. She was not like the pampered women back East who were fashionably weak and dependent. She led a hard life and loved it because she traveled with her husband, whom she loved.

The Custer group left Yankton one fall day to travel to a new post five hundred miles away. At a speed of 4 miles an hour that trip took quite a few days. At night the travelers would sit in a circle around the campfire, sing, and tell scary stories. Mrs. Custer and the other women compared notes on such things as how to improve their recipe for beaver tail, which wasn't bad eating, but just had too much fat.

Traveling across the plains was an entirely new life compared to traveling in the East. The Indians were only a small part of the problem. When the wind blew, the alkali sand clogged the traveler's throat, parched his lips, and made his eyes sting. At night there were mosquitoes to keep him from sleeping. Since there was no wood, it was very hard to start fires. Buffalo chips could be used, but by 1876 buffalo were getting hard to find—and so were their chips. The hardest part was not finding water to drink. Even where there was a river, the thirsty traveler had to wait a while for the mud to settle to the bottom of his cup.

It is not surprising that in 1876 people were seriously thinking about traveling in the air. Aeronauts were planning on balloons though, not airplanes. One aeronaut was so anxious to go up faster that he threw out everything he had in his basket to make his balloon rise more rapidly. Fortunately he did not go up too high and he came down in one piece—more or less. Some aeronauts were not so lucky. A professor claimed he could fly to England by following the Gulf Stream, drifting in his balloon in the warm air. When last heard from, he was doing just that. There was a lot of mystery connected with flying-ship inventions because each man wanted to be the first and only inventor of The Flying Ship.

Wilbur Wright was nine years old and his little brother, Orville, was five when on the next-to-last day of 1876 a man named W. J. Lewis flew over Manhattan in a flying machine that "scientific gentlemen pronounce a decided wonder." The newspaper continued by saying that this flying machine could eventually go 100 miles an hour. What was even more surprising was that it flew in the direction in which it was pointed. But evidently only the scientific men were impressed, because Mr. Lewis' flying machine was forgotten . . . almost. Recently a designer and aerodynamicist from the Grumman Aerospace Corporation took a good look at Mr. Lewis' designs. The goofy-looking flying machine is not at all unlike a Piasecki type of helicopter, and as the newspaper stated, W. J. Lewis really did succeed in flying it. The only way in which he failed was to convince people that something terribly important had happened that cold day in 1876.

Not only did this "airplane" fly, but a present-day aerodynamicist says its design is very much like a modern Piasecki helicopter

8

WHERE TO LIVE—
CITY OR COUNTRY?

Now doth the little onion
Poke up its little head
And the restless little radish
Stretch in its little bed.

—From a Pennsylvania
newspaper, May 1876

For probably the last time in world history there was plenty of space in the United States in 1876. Cities were not too large yet and the rural areas had no boundaries. The greatest number of people were living in the country.

It was a new spring and the farmers were hoping for a little more cooperation from nature. For the past two years, the best of the crops had gone to the grasshoppers. They had swarmed out of the skies during the summer of 1874 in hordes up to 150 miles wide by 100 miles long and had eaten everything in sight. Farmers' wives rushed out to hide a few of their precious foods under blankets, only to find that grasshoppers-on-the-rampage also ate blankets. They ate the leather harness parts, window curtains, and even the wooden hoe handles that were salty from the sweat of human hands. One day so many slippery grasshopper bodies were jam-packed across the railroad tracks that the wheels of a train spun because they could not get enough traction to move forward.

By the summer of 1875, every child in the countryside was collecting dead grasshopper bodies in bushel baskets. Some states paid up to 50 cents a bushel for bodies of "Public Enemy #1." Minnesota actually went bankrupt trying to pay for all the basketfuls. Farmers counted on dead grasshoppers to help make up their losses. Sometimes they were arrested for "poaching" grasshoppers on other farms. "Just knock them off the branches and they will fall on their heads and be killed," said a local newspaper. But it took much more than that to kill a grasshopper. At last, in the spring of 1876, the papers noted that grasshopper eggs were being eaten by a tiny red insect. Whatever the red insect was, it was the hero-of-the-year.

The country general store was the center of social life in rural America. Since the coming of the railroads, wandering peddlers had given way to two new types of salesmen. First, there were the "manufacturer's agents." They sold the larger items such as sewing machines, parlor organs, washing machines, and new kinds of kerosene lamps. They showed up about once a year at each country store to leave a sample and show the storekeeper how to work it. Then there were the "drummers." They sent postals to storekeepers to let them know which day they would arrive in town to exhibit the newest thing in crockery, crackers, tobacco, and other products. Important train reading for a drummer was *Jokes and Anecdotes for Railroad Travelers and Fun Lovers.* When the drummer came to town the storekeeper knew he would hear a lot of new jokes to tell his customers. Also he would hear the latest news and gossip from other towns on the drummer's route.

Children always found something new at the store—a new toy or book, new trading cards left by the drummers, and colorful posters the grocer might let them take home. At the end of the year there was the new almanac put out by the patent medicine people with new jokes and stories. Then there were the smells—of sour pickles, freshly ground coffee, pound bars of soap, and fish packed in brine. It was even fun to count the dead flies stuck on the arsenic-coated curl of sticky flypaper. Sometimes the storekeeper might offer a cracker from the barrel or a piece of candy. A child with a penny to spend on candy could come home with a whole bag—corn kisses,

*Anything from a cradle to a coffin could be bought
at the country general store*

hearts, Gibraltars, cinnamon red-hots, lemon gumdrops, cockles, Zanzibars, and fortune candies.

A person could buy anything from a cradle to a coffin at the general store. New items came in every day—like the new celluloid collars for men's shirts which never wore out as did the old unwashable paper collars. A lady could even find hoops, although they had been out of style for years.

Mail was not delivered to homes in the country. People just stopped in at the general store to see if any letters had come for them or to mail letters out. The storekeeper's wife was often the postmistress. It cost 3 cents to mail a half-ounce letter and one cent to mail a newspaper. Letters to foreign countries cost anywhere from 4 cents (open mail to England) up to 9 cents to France. Packages were delivered by American Railway Express in the East and by Wells, Fargo and Company west of the Mississippi River.

Most grocery items—such as molasses, oatmeal, and sugar—came to the store in heavy barrels or crates made of wood. A new machine was now turning out paper bags by the thousands, although it was not always working right. The "fast check out counter" was unheard of in a country store. Tea was weighed out on a tea scale, then wrapped in white paper and tied with red-and-white striped "tea twine." Sugar was weighed on heavier scales and the lumps broken up, then it was wrapped in heavy paper and tied with another kind of string. Before 1876 very few groceries came already wrapped in small packages. That was a new idea introduced during the Centennial year. Before then almost everything had to be measured and put in a sack or wrapped in paper. When the grocer opened his cash drawer, a steel gong sounded—to make sure no one except the grocer opened it.

Storekeepers were not always honest themselves. Every customer thought the grocer held out on him a little, but in many cases some of his groceries had already been "stretched a little" before they even reached the store. The sugar barrel was not always filled with pure sugar, for example. The farmers were not always so honest, either. One country store owner ran into the farmer who had sold him a supply of balls of butter.

"You know, Zeb," said the storekeeper, "those balls of butter you sold me last week were all three ounces short of being a pound."

"Can't be!" said the farmer. "They had to weigh exactly a pound, because I used for a weight the one-pound bar of soap you sold me the week before."

During the winter, the store was heated by a little stove called a "spit and sizzle." A few local people were always in the store, just relaxing or with a chessboard balanced on their knees. The latest news was repeated for each new arrival—who was married, who had a baby, what boy was courting which girl, and when the next square dance was to be held at the Grange hall.

The Grange was an important part of the farmer's life. The Federal Bureau of Agriculture had sent Oliver Hudson Kelley all over the country to see what could be done to help farmers. His suggestion was to start local Grange units—all tied together in the National Grange of the Patrons of Husbandry. But the Granges were a great deal more than a social group. Immediately they began helping the farmer to organize against the railroads. Railroads had been charging different prices to everyone. A large corporation did not pay as much to have its products shipped as did a poor little farmer. Working together in their Granges, farmers managed to have laws passed that would help them. Even the farmers' wives benefited from the Grange wives' meetings, where they learned sewing, cooking, canning, and other helpful women's work. The young people counted on the Grange socials to get acquainted with other young people living on farms.

Aaron Montgomery Ward was getting his start about the same time as the Granges. He had once been a country storekeeper and was paid $6 a month, but by 1876 he worked for a large department store, and it was his job to sell goods to country stores. He knew that the farmers were paying very high prices at their local stores, but they had no choice. Ward thought that he could sell goods to farmers a better way. He would write a catalog with the price of each item beside it. Then the farmer could send his money and Ward would mail back what the farmer wanted. Ward tied in his idea with the new Granges—when more people got together to

The Grange meeting in 1876 was the only way farmers could get together to control a common enemy like the railroads

order what they wanted, their goods were shipped all together to one address more cheaply. The result was a great saving for farmers—and the start of the mail-order business.

Ward's catalog had almost four thousand items in it by 1876. Country people called it their "Wish Book." For the first time, farmers enjoyed a privilege only city folk had had before—they could get their money back if they did not like what they bought. At first men had been afraid to order "store-boughten" suits. Until the War Between the States, tailors thought that everyone was a

Stylish farmers wore the "Grange Hat" offered through the new Montgomery Ward catalog

different size and shape. But uniform makers soon noticed that certain combinations of measurements went together. Men with a 36-inch waist usually wore trousers that were 30 inches long on the inside seam. Ward's catalog said that their merchandise would "nine times out of ten give you a fit"—and the company offered the money back if the garment failed to fit.

Farmers were about to win another battle—this one with cattle. Until 1874, herds of cattle on their way to the railroad terminals could trample down any fence a human could build. In most prairie country there were no trees to build log fences such as those around the fields east of the Mississippi River. And there were no stones to build rock walls like those in New England. Then two farmers in Illinois invented barbed wire. The wire could be made cheaply enough so that even owners of large farms could fence in their land.

Perhaps barbed wire would not have caught on so quickly if it had not been for a very unusual salesman named John W. "Bet-a-Million" Gates. His way of selling the wire was to pen thirty angry steers in a small area with barbed-wire fencing. Ordinarily few people would have noticed the pen. But this one was in the very center of San Antonio, Texas. Gates sold ten thousand pounds of wire the next year.

In 1876 there were none of the round silos that are so familiar on farms today. And dairy cows gave very little milk in cold climates. In Europe, some farmers had dug pits in the ground, filled them with grain and covered them over. A lot of the grain spoiled with such treatment, but the farmers seemed to think having extra grain and grasses during the winter had helped increase the milk supply.

In 1873, an Illinois farmer named Fred Hatch built himself a square silo above the ground. His grain lasted better, but all the grasses stored near the corners of his square silo had spoiled because of exposure to the air. It would be another six years before someone built a round silo.

Someone was always thinking of improvements for McCormick's reaper, and in 1876 Sylvanus J. Locke had invented a self-binder. A belt caught the grain after it was cut, gathered it and tied it with wire into bundles. But it still took a man sixty-four hours to prepare one acre of soil for planting, plant the seed, and, after it was ripe, cut and bind it. Today it takes less than three hours.

Taking care of the animals was one job that kept young people busy around a farm. Stray cows had to be advertised in the paper if they were worth over $20. One businessman was always losing his cows. He was a young lawyer from Texas who had inherited four hundred cows in payment of a debt. He had no idea what to do with them and never even got around to branding them as his own.

"Whose cows are those on our ranch?" other cattlemen were asking every few days.

After a quick inspection for a brand, the foreman would say, "I guess they're Maverick's." He meant that they belonged to the lawyer Samuel A. Maverick. By 1876 every stray cow or steer anywhere in the country was called a maverick.

After the War Between the States, Texas beef was worth a great deal more in the Northern markets. The cattle had to be taken northward to a cow town on the railroad line. This meant plenty of jobs for men who could take the rough life. At least five thousand cowboys in the Southwest in 1876 were Negroes. The best black riders came from the South—probably because these men never had had a chance to ride in carriages, like the slave owners, but rode horses instead. When it came to riding a bronco with "a bellyful of bedsprings," the black riders were often the best.

Country people could not feed all their animals during a hard winter, so plans had to be made to butcher the ones that could be spared. Not a portion could be wasted. Pork was salted and packed into barrels—that way it could last about a year. Some meat was pickled. Hams, sausage, and bacon were smoked. Some was dried. "Jerky" was made by cutting lean venison or beef into one-inch-wide strips and drying them in the sun until they were as stiff as rawhide. Jerky was perfect to slip into a pocket and take along on a trip. It could also be added to soups.

Intestines were cleaned out and stuffed with sausage meat. Bladders were used as a container for oil paint or tobacco. Glue and a dressing for leather were made from hooves. Horns and antlers could be turned into spoons, combs, cups, lantern panes, powder horns, tool handles, buttons, hunting horns, and dozens of other implements. Shoes could be stitched with the sinews. Fats and oils were used to make tallow for candles, lamp fuel, lard and cooking oil, or soap. The furry pelts made robes or jackets. Hides were turned into shoes, boots, harness, saddlery, snowshoes, parchment and vellum, fire buckets, or even a traveling chest.

Young people learned early to value wood. "Wood warms a man twice," was the old saying. "It warms him once when he cuts it and again when he burns it." In the early spring, shingles were made when the frost made splitting the wood easier.

Wheel spokes or barrels made from unseasoned lumber would fall apart. If a woodworker did not season the end of the wooden handle that fit into the metal part, the ax head would fly off its handle. The bark of wild chestnut trees peeled off intact and could be used to make a pipe for running water. A ferryboat or floating bridge built of chestnut or locust logs would not rot in water. An oak sapling could be pulled down to the ground, allowed to spring back slowly—and the force would provide enough power to turn a hand lathe. A wagon part made of ash would break easily, because the wood of the ash tree was not flexible. Sourwood made the best runners for sleds when children had to build their own.

Country dwellers had their own ways to tell the weather. Fish swimming near the surface of a pond, frogs croaking more than usual, a pale moon with hazy edges, swallows flying low and dipping their wings in water, chickens fluttering in dust, and moles throwing up more dirt around their holes meant rain. Enough blue sky showing "to make a Dutchman a pair of breeches" meant that the clouds would soon disappear. A fiery red moon and falling stars meant a windy day coming. Everyone knew: "An evening red and a morning gray will set the traveler on his way . . . but evening gray and morning red will pour down rain on the pilgrim's head."

Bad weather did not bother the farmer so much as planting or harvesting his crops at the wrong times. As a rule, root crops were planted when the moon was dark. Crops that yielded above ground, such as corn, were planted in the new moon or while the moon was getting larger. Full moons were for harvesting.

Any man with a set of muscles and a few dollars could hardly resist the offers in his newspapers during the spring of 1876.

"Prairie lands—the last chance for good agricultural lands on 10 years' credit at 6% interest. Don't run any risks, but go to a country that has proved to be good—Iowa!"

"Lands for sale in southwest Missouri! From $2.50 to $10 an acre. Free transportation furnished purchasers."

"HO! FOR CALIFORNIA! The Laborer's Paradise. Salubrious Climate. Fertile Soil. Large Labor returns. No Severe Winters. No Lost Time. No blights nor insect pests."

Thousands of people moved westward, but many others moved into cities where life appeared to be filled with luxuries. The best-fed people in 1876 lived along the Atlantic Coast. Every morning the newspapers announced what ships were docking and what cargo would be unloaded that day.

"Potatoes are almost perfect now," said a New York City paper early in July. "Also green peas, string beans, tomatoes, cucumbers, white turnips, red and black raspberries, cherries, currants, gooseberries, watermelons from Georgia, salmon from Maine." Other tempting morsels for city breakfasts ranged from little Jamaican butter-birds to Southern rice buntings.

City life had always begun on the waterfront, but in 1876 the waterfront was about to lose its importance as the center of activity because of the railroads.

Almost every inch of space along the docks was filled with steamships and sailing ships. When there was not enough space, some ships had to anchor in the rivers and wait their turn to be unloaded at the docks. There were no buoys or radar to show captains where the channel was or where there were hidden shoals. Every ship tried to stay in the middle of the river, where it was usually deepest.

Small ships, called "the hucksters of the dock," carried food, water, and small goods out to the larger ships anchored offshore. The hucksters could slip easily and quickly through the narrow spaces between the bigger ships. An oyster sloop might tie up at an available space at a dock, and a dozen smaller boats would hitch themselves onto it. Their crews tramped across the sloop's deck as though it were part of the dock, carrying their products back and forth.

Ferryboats steamed back and forth constantly from one shore to the other. There were very few bridges across large rivers. The ones built of iron were rusting, and now engineers wanted to build bridges of steel, like the big new bridge at St. Louis. But who needed bridges as long as there were plenty of ferryboats? Only in places where there were railroads were bridges really necessary. But in the winter of 1875–1876 there was so much ice that for weeks the ferries could not run. People in Brooklyn could not even get across the river to New York City. At last the experts agreed to go ahead and build the Brooklyn Bridge.

Large white side-wheelers took passengers and goods upriver to smaller cities. Canalboats loaded with coal came down from the coal regions. Special river and harbor police boats were connected with the new "police telegraph" in large port cities. Word of an accident on the river or of a sinking was flashed over the telegraph to the police boats, and they sped to the scene. Every large port also had its revenue cutters—sailing ships that often came to the rescue. Someday they would be called the Coast Guard.

Cities were not only moving back from the waterfront, but they were going *up!* Philadelphia citizens were about to lay the cornerstone for their new city hall, and it was going to be a mile back from the docks. It was also to be the tallest building in the world. Besides having seven floors of offices, there would be a tower topped by a statue of William Penn. Just the statue alone would be higher than a three-story house!

Since steel was being used for bridges, architects talked of using steel to build frameworks for even high buildings. A few years before, people would have laughed at such a thought because, no matter how high a building was, a person could climb just so many flights of steps. But in 1876, Mr. Otis was showing an elevator at the Centennial, and suddenly architects saw all kinds of possibilities. "When the 9th story may be reached by a swift moving steam elevator," said one builder, "every objection that might exist against this great height is removed." The air was much cleaner nine floors up from the dusty street. It was quieter and the light was better too.

Meanwhile, city streets were becoming as crowded as the rivers. Streets used by horsecars were kept up better than most and were well graded. Snow was shoveled off the tracks and holes in the road repaired immediately so the horses could get through. For this reason, most carriage drivers preferred going along the horsecar tracks where they had the right of way over traffic coming down the railway from the opposite direction. Actually, the horsecars had the first right of way, but since they could travel only 6 miles an hour, it was easy for a carriage driver to whip around either side of the cars and back onto the track in front. There was a speed limit. No one was allowed to "ride a horse or drive one attached to a carriage, wagon, cart, or any other vehicle at a gallop" and all drivers must slow down to a walking pace when crossing a bridge. Vehicles could stop only at the far right hand side of a street, and drivers were fined $5 for going on a footway (sidewalk) whether it was "bricked, planked or paved."

There were plenty of accidents. Carriage wheels could fly off at high speeds and drivers were often thrown out of their vehicles. A horse standing still at a corner could be suddenly frightened by any unexpected noise and start up so fast that a driver might tumble right off his seat.

Cities were prepared for these emergencies. The injured man was picked up and jostled between two carriers to the hospital. If he was lucky enough to fall where there was a stretcher handy, he got a ride. A very few cities at that time had something called an ambulance such as the army had used during the War Between the States to carry wounded men. It was a wagon with fast horses and had a place to put the stretchers inside. The idea was just to get the victim to the hospital fast—not comfortably. A simple fracture might be a lot worse by the time the patient arrived.

Cities had public transportation called horsecars or street railroads. They charged 25 cents for four rides. Usually each line was a different color. The rider could transfer free to a line of the same color, but if he transferred to one of the competitor's horsecar lines, he paid 2 cents. Hacks, like our taxicabs, were expensive—75 cents a mile for one passenger and $1.25 for two. Sometimes it was cheaper to rent a carriage for $1.50 an hour from a livery stable. Railroad cars were the best way to travel longer distances. When the passengers got off their trains in the city, hotel omnibuses—also pulled by horses—were parked outside waiting to take them to the front doors of the best hotels in town.

Many towns that a person cannot reach by public transportation today were simple to get to in 1876 via stagecoach, railroad, horse, or boat. Some towns important enough to have a train station then are almost forgotten today. The "county seat" is one of these. A hundred years ago, the county seat was "the big city" to the thousands of country people who lived in that county. The traveling judge came there to hold court during certain weeks that were announced in advance in the newspapers. So did traveling doctors and dentists.

One of the big advantages of living in the city was that it had paved sidewalks—sometimes. For a woman wearing a long skirt, walking could be very messy. Usually city streets had bricks or else stone or wooden blocks cut into squares and fitted into place. There were no concrete streets or sidewalks yet because no one had agreed on the recipe to make concrete. Each company had its own formula and no two concrete blocks turned out the same! Streets were usually muddy and dirty, even in large cities. Muddy tracks and ruts were smoothed out of dirt roads by a horse pulling a square log sideways.

The city was where the action was. Many had theaters, and the best actors and actresses traveled around the nation to appear in them. *Our American Cousin* was a play everyone wanted to see—not because it was the best play of the year but because Abraham Lincoln had been shot watching a performance of it. Some of the best plays of the year were considered shocking then. Some talked about unmentionable subjects such as divorce. Some even used bad words, for example, "leg" instead of "limb." Since no lady or gentleman would ever use the word "leg," even to ask for a chicken leg at dinner, the character of the play was labeled "common" by his use of the wrong word. Plays were becoming too realistic, parents thought, and young people were advised to stay away from theaters.

One of the special events of the year was the appearance of the Jubilee Singers. By now, there were several groups, all claiming to be former slaves and singing slave songs. The original singers had come from Fisk University in 1871 as a group of students trying to

WALNUT STREET THEATRE.

Proprietor and Director,   Mr. J. S. Clarke
Managers,   -   -   -   Mr. J. S. Clarke, Mr. G. K. Goodwin

This Monday Evening, June 5, 1876,
MR. SOTHERN,
Will appear in his celebrated part of **LORD DUNDREARY**,
His original character, written and created by himself, and acted
by him in America and Europe over 4000 times, in Tom
Taylor's three-act Comedy, entitled

OUR AMERICAN COUSIN

Assisted by the Talented Young Artiste,
MISS LINDA DIETZ,
Of the Theatre Royal, Haymarket, London, who has been specially
engaged to support Mr. Sothern.

MR. CHARLES WALCOT   as   ASA TRENCHARD

UNPARALLELED CAST, WHICH INCLUDES
MR. SOTHERN,   -   -   - Lord Dundreary
Created and written by himself.

Charles Walcot.. ....as............................Asa Trenchard
W. H. Bailey.........................as..............Sir Edward Trenchard
Sam Hemple.........................as.........................Binney
H. E. Meredith ....as...........................Abel Murcott
Roland Reed.........................as.........................Buddicombe
B. W. Turner.........................as.........................Richard Coyle
Atkins Lawrence.........................as.............Lieut. Vernon, R. N
Willis H. Page.........................as.........................Captain De Boots
Mrs. Charles Walcot.........................as.........................May Meredith
Miss Linda Dietz.........................as.........................Georgina
[From the Haymarket Theatre, London, her first appearance in this city.]
Mrs. T. A. Creese ....as.........................Florence Trenchard
Mrs. W. A. Chapman ....as ....Mrs. Montchessington
Miss Nellie Barbour.........................as ....Augusta

In the course of the piece, Mr. SOTHERN will introduce the reading of BROTHER
SAM'S LETTER. Received nightly with the unprecedented compliment of a Triple
Encore. The piece ends with a New Rhyming Tag, which the audience are respect-
fully requested not to interrupt by rising from their seats.

Act I.   Sir Edward Trenchard's House.
     Act II.   Sir Edward Trenchard's Library.
Act III.   The Dairy.   Act IV.   Drawing-Room in Trenchard Mansion

Saturday Afternoon, Mr. Sothern as Lord Dundreary.

In active preparation, John Brougham's Great Historical Extravaganza

COLUMBUS RECONSTRUCTED,
Which will be produced with Beautiful and Appropriate Scenery,
Intricate Military Evolutions, by a Corps of over Fifty Young
Ladies, Original Local Songs, Trios, Choruses, and every
attention to detail.   Engagement of the Wonderful Mimic,
Mr. N. C. GOODWIN.

The Piano used at this Theatre is from the Establishment of James Bellak, 279 and
281 South Fifth street

The Furniture used at this Theatre is from the Establishment of T. A. McClelland
1219 Chestnut street.

Mr. C. K. Burns, Treasurer | Chas. Walcot, Stage Manager | J. P. Deuel, Prompter

Park Theatre, Broadway and 22nd St, New York, Summer Season,
The new version of Uncle Tom's Cabin, with Georgia Jubilee
Singers, and Mrs G. C. Howard as Topsey.

Wallack's Theatre, Broadway, New York, Summer Season, Mr. and
Mrs. W. J. Florence in their Great Success, the "Mighty Dollar."

The audience that attended Our American Cousin *on June 5,
1876, saw Edward A. Sothern play a part he had written
himself and performed over 4,000 times*

earn money for their college, one of the few existing for black students. They were so successful, especially in the North where people had never heard the old plantation melodies, that they earned over $150,000 for their school. They also started a new kind of folk music in the United States.

The Jubilee Singers were the only Negroes many Northerners ever saw. Black people were moving northward in 1876, but not yet in great numbers. Most of the former slaves had no money to move, and before they took their chances, they were waiting to hear from their friends who had already moved up to the cities. Most of them had been able to find homes only in the ugliest sections of town.

Crime in 1876 ran from what the newspapers called "dastardly deeds," such as striking a horse or stealing, to murder and kidnapping. Police were still trying to find the kidnappers of a little four-year-old boy, Charley Ross, who had been stolen from his millionaire father's home a few years earlier. Charley was never found. One man dropped "an infernal machine," which was a homemade bomb, into his neighbor's coal chute. The unfortunate neighbor discovered it by chance when shoveling the coal into his furnace. Every age has its vicious characters.

Many of the "criminals" of that year would not even be taken to a police station today for what they did. Mary Hicks, age seventeen, spent Christmas and the next two months in the House of Correction. She had been out looking for a job one night in November when a citizen took her "for her own good" to the police. Frank Johnson was a farm boy of eighteen. He had come to the big city of Philadelphia five days earlier to find out how the other half lived. But the city cost a lot more than Frank had ever dreamed. He ran out of money and was arrested for begging on January 8. He was sentenced to three months in jail, but he escaped. Jim Carr was a sixteen-year-old who could not get along with his father. Papa had him arrested and Jim would have spent the next nine months "being corrected" if he too had not escaped.

What scared people most in the city was not crime, but fires. In the old days, a bucket brigade could put out a fire in a low house, but now most city buildings were four stories high. Ladders were not long enough, and there was not sufficient pressure behind the

Before the days of uniforms and paid fire departments, this crew put out fires with their 1863 Amoskeag steamer

water to make it shoot up high enough. Rival firefighting companies used to reach the scene of a fire and then fight over which of them would put the fire out.

On October 8, 1871, the Chicago Fire destroyed nearly $200,000,000 worth of property and killed over 250 people. The very same night another drastic forest fire wiped out many small towns near Peshtigo, Wisconsin. Only one year later, the city of Boston had its worst fire. This time most of the problem had been with the horses that pulled the fire engines—they were sick with the "epizootic," and the only engines to reach the fire had to be pulled by men.

The Chicago Fire in 1871 prompted many changes in firefighting during the next five years

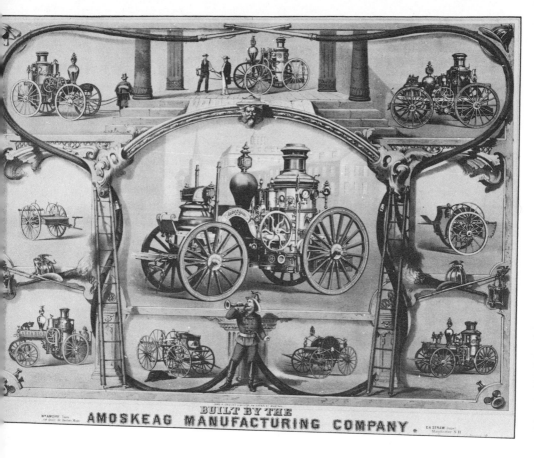

The most modern firefighting equipment was displayed at the Centennial

Because of those disastrous fires, most cities had installed paid fire departments and replaced the old hand fire engines with steam engines. These were still pulled by horses, but with the steam these engines could build up more water pressure. New fire alarms were put on the streets so that any citizen could turn in an alarm, rather than first having to find a policeman who had a key to turn on an alarm. The Hayes aerial ladder, called "the big stick," was proving to be a wonderful invention. Attached to a wagon as a firm base, the ladder could be raised mechanically.

A few inventions did not turn out so well. One was the new fireman's suit that was to allow him to walk safely through the hottest fire. A pipe ran up his back and through his helmet, pouring water down over him constantly. It did not work, but a new way to stop fire in a room was successful. From a heavy water tank on the roof of a building, water ran down through pipes into various rooms. A valve was opened when a fire was started. That was the first sprinkler system, but it needed a person to turn it on.

Most of the activity in cities was commerce. In the wee hours of the morning, the "milk train" brought in the fresh milk from the country. City inspectors had taken to inspecting milk because companies added water to make the milk go farther. One 1876 joke was told about a milkman knocking on the Joneses' door to ask where their next-door neighbors had gone.

"Why, the Kellys moved a week ago," said Mr. Jones.

"But he owed me money for milk," groaned the milkman. "I figure he owes me about $2.48."

"Well, it's not really that much loss to you," said Jones. "Figuring about 20 percent of that milk was water, Mr. Kelly really owes you only about $1.98."

"But that was the worst of it," the sad milkman admitted. "They were new customers and I hadn't begun to water their milk yet. They were getting pure milk!"

Peddlers roamed the streets with carts and knocked on doors selling goods. Two men in the candle business, named Procter and Gamble, sold twenty-four kinds of soap in addition to their candles. A man selling his coffee door to door managed to talk a Maxwell House hotel cook into buying some regularly. The coffee salesman named it for the hotel.

In Pittsburgh, Pennsylvania, a young man named H. J. Heinz was selling horseradish door to door. He had put his product in a glass jar so that his customers could see what they were buying. But already that year he was close to bankruptcy. He had planned to sell pickles, so he had contracted for bushels of cucumbers to make them. Unfortunately, the year he ordered the cucumbers was a terrible year for growing them, and they cost an unbelievable 60 cents a bushel. The next year, cucumbers were growing all over and the price was way down, but Heinz had to pay the high price he had contracted for. He was broke now, but still struggling. In fact, he was selling catsup, a new product he hoped would help get him back on his feet.

The largest department store in the world was the Cast Iron Palace in New York. It was eight stories high and covered a whole city block. Department stores were a new idea. Instead of shopping in dozens of small stores to buy what she wanted, a woman could find almost everything under one roof. In Philadelphia, John Wanamaker bought an old railroad freight depot and opened the Wanamaker Grand Depot. In Chicago, Marshall Field opened his new store after being nearly ruined by the fire five years before.

————•◆•————

Crowds hurried by foot, carriage, and horsecar to the opening of the Wanamaker Grand Depot department store

Store owners in 1876 often cheated by selling the same goods at several different prices. The customer was supposed to haggle over the price, saying, "No, that's too expensive," before the shopkeeper would come down in price. The best arguer got the best price. But department stores had a one-price policy. What was even more surprising to customers was that now, if they were not satisfied, they could get their money back. At Marshall Field's store, there was even a policy that "The customer is always right."

The cash register had not been invented and "cash drawers" were busy. People had a lot of coins to jingle in their pockets. Some still had half-cent pieces, although they had not been issued since 1857. There were one-cent pieces, two-cent pieces, three-cent pieces, and a half-dime that was a miniature of a dime. The dime was the same size as it is today. There was a twenty-cent piece smaller than a quarter, and a twenty-five-cent piece that was called a quarter dollar. The half dollar was also the same size as it is today. "Greenbacks" were U.S. treasury notes that did not have either gold or silver behind them—only promises of the Government to pay. A person was luckier to have a gold certificate, made of paper but backed by gold. Gold was the basic monetary unit of the United States and no silver dollars had been issued since 1873. The silver producers did not like this, and in a few years they would have the country back on silver. But by 1876, people liked the lightweight paper dollars better than the old heavy silver ones.

Paper money was becoming popular in 1876 with men who disliked carrying heavy coins in their pockets

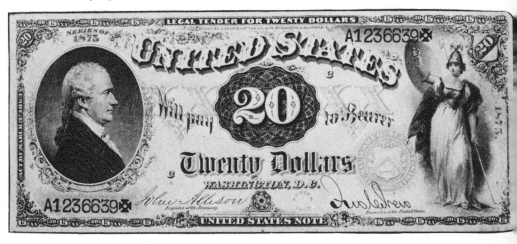

Communication was sometimes better than it is today. A letter dropped in a Philadelphia letter box on Friday morning would arrive in Baltimore, Maryland, that same afternoon via the morning steamship which traveled through the Chesapeake and Delaware Canal. A "drop letter," mailed to someone within the city, cost only 2 cents. Penny postals were new within the last few years and they started a new fad among children—to see who could write the most words on one.

An 1876 newspaper told about the "wonderful invention" of Professor Alexander Graham Bell, but it did not mean his telephone. He had been astounding telegraph operators by sending musical sounds so well over electrified wires that the operators could even recognize "America" and "Auld Lang Syne." So far, though, only two people could hear the sounds at a time. The only use for this invention that the newspaper could foresee was that someday an audience in a New York City music hall might be able to listen to a singer who was performing in Boston.

But Bell had bigger ideas. In 1876 he had applied for a patent on his new voice telegraphy invention that he was showing at the Centennial. For the first time voices could be understood—and the speakers identified. In a year there would be eight hundred telephones in the United States.

The telephone was not the only luxury about to thrill city dwellers. One day in 1875, *Appleton's Journal*, reported: "That our readers may be prepared for any subsequent revelations on the subject, Mr. Edison of Newark claims to have discovered either a new force or a modification of an electric-force which, if it accomplishes half that is claimed for it, will effect far more for the cause of progress than we dare to conceive."

At just about the same time, Edison was joined by Lewis Latimer, a young black electrical engineer who had helped Bell by making drawings of the telephone when Bell had applied for a patent. But it would be three years before Latimer and Edison would hit upon the right material to use in making a light bulb that would burn longer than forty hours. At the moment Edison's laboratory was the busiest place in town. Other inventions poured out of it, but not the light bulb yet.

The details in this painting of Alexander Graham Bell and his first telephone were supplied by a sketch made by Bell's assistant, Thomas A. Watson. The inventor was twenty-nine, working in an attic at 109 Court Street, Boston

Meanwhile more and more people began moving into the city. Tenements started looking alarmingly unhealthy. Immigrants were beginning to crowd in from other countries and they tended to settle in cities where there were other immigrants from their homelands. Soon there were thousands of people who really did not want to be either in the city or in the country—just sort of on the edge where they might have the advantages of both. They would start the suburbs someday—but not in 1876.

9

THE CENTENNIAL EXHIBITION AND OTHER SPECIAL DAYS

At ten o'clock on New Year's Eve, Joel Bailey hired a carriage for himself and his wife. He knew that this night was going to be a wild one, so he was taking no chances on driving his own carriage among the crowds gathered in the center of Philadelphia.

The celebrators had not even waited for the new year to come. All the past summer, special events had been going on in cities remembered for battles a hundred years before. Lexington and Concord had had their special day on April 19, 1875. Then Bostonians had held a special ceremony at Bunker Hill in June. Many Southern troops had come to the North for the occasion, and the Bostonians were touched to have them there. The War Between the States was only ten years past, and feelings were still tender.

Now it was almost the first day of the Centennial year. As the Baileys climbed into their rented carriage, they were already awed by the great crowds in the streets around them. Joel was glad he had hired a driver to handle the horses. People packed the streets as thickly as they did the sidewalks. In spite of the damp, cold air, hundreds were marching on Broad and Chestnut Streets in colorful costumes, playing music with every instrument that could be carried easily.

Every building in the city was lighted up from the inside by gaslights and from the outside by flares. Some lights were almost blinding white, but many were in colors. Red, white, and blue lights were everywhere. At Carpenters' Hall, gas jets spelled out "The Nation's Birthplace." Theaters were lighted with red, white, and blue globes. Calcium lights placed in windows across the way illuminated storefronts as brightly as day. A short way from Independence Hall was a giant picture of Thomas Jefferson signing the Declaration of Independence.

Suddenly at midnight every bell in the city chimed. Shots from cannons and muskets rang out as fast as human hands could do the reloading. Every steamship, tugboat, and locomotive blew its steam whistle. Bells rang out at Independence Hall: 1-7-7-6, 1-8-7-6, and then one hundred peals. The nation's one hundredth year had begun.

"The whole city sounded like an immense beehive," said one of the Baileys' neighbors.

Police tried shoving the crowd back from the center of the streets, but they had an impossible job.

"The crowd was simply terrible to be in," said Mrs. Bailey. "We had to stop the horses several times to let the crowd pack in a little tighter."

Only a few minutes after the Baileys' carriage pulled through the worst of the traffic jam, the happy jostling mob won their tussle with the police. For more than an hour, not a single carriage could get down Chestnut Street to Independence Hall, where most of the evening's excitement was to take place. The carriages were just pushed along on waves of people. By the time the parades were over and the year 1876 had been properly welcomed, the Baileys arrived home rumpled and exhausted.

"This New Year's Eve was a particularly lively one," Mrs. Bailey wrote in her diary before she fell asleep. "We were glad to get away."

The next morning many of the revelers were still out in the streets even though it was misty and cold. Clowns, Indians, and many other costumed marchers looked much the worse for wear. But their music was still heard in the streets. The Baileys took their little girl Susan out to watch the parades, not knowing that they were watching the beginning of a special Philadelphia event that would still be taking place one hundred New Year's Days later—the Mummers Parade.

Long before the Centennial grounds in Fairmount Park were ready to open, people began driving their carriages out there on a Sunday afternoon just to see how things were coming along. When the weather was dry, the dust whirled through the roads in every direction. There were no fences around the site, and people roamed in and out of the great buildings that were being finished.

Horticultural Hall had been half finished before Christmas and the Centennial committee was frantic. It had no money to finish the second half. In fact, there was no money to finish the Centennial at all. What could they do? They invited President Ulysses S. Grant and several other Washington dignitaries to dinner. The feast was held in the giant iron-and-glass Horticultural Hall. After dessert, the President and his party were invited to take a tour of the "rest of the building." As they stepped over piles of iron, kegs of nails, and other rubble, they slowly got the idea. The committee chairman pointed out to the group where all the rest of the buildings would soon be—provided the committee ever got any money to complete their ambitious project.

It was a ticklish situation for the President to ask Congress to help with money for what was really a private enterprise. It was not really a project that public funds should be paying for. But Congress agreed with President Grant that the depression of 1873 had left everyone in the country feeling discouraged. Perhaps this Centennial would be just the lift they all needed. The vote was close, but on January 25, 1876, the Centennial committee received $1,500,000 to finish the exhibition halls. There were only three months and a few days to finish everything before the opening on May 10. The workmen labored day and night—but not on Sundays. That would have been breaking the Sabbath.

Everywhere were stacks of lumber, iron, glass, empty crates, and swarms of workmen. Wagonloads of supplies hurtled in every direction on the rutted, muddy roads throughout the grounds. But it was the workmen from other countries who fascinated the American audiences the most.

Chinese workmen wore their Oriental clothes. None of the rules of etiquette, so strictly observed with people of one's own "class," applied to foreigners. Everyone stared rudely at the Orientals and made remarks about them. Children followed them in the streets and jeered to make them turn around. Every day large groups of Americans watched the Japanese workmen as they began building the Japanese pavilion.

"Their tools are different from ours!" said one newspaper. The Japanese used an ink line instead of a chalk line to mark their walls. Each carpenter wore a sash around his waist to hold his tools and also a small wicker basket for nails. Even their nails had to be examined by the curious spectators. When they planed lumber, instead of pushing their planes away from them they pulled the planes toward them. Instead of large saws, they had some with very thin blades and small, sharp teeth. Americans in 1876 were not at all worldly. Most thought that their own way of doing things was the only way. The Centennial was going to change some of their provincial thinking. "The Oriental workmen are not as clumsy as you might think from their odd tools," the newspaper admitted.

While the winter winds blew and snow packed in the Northern towns until spring, people had to go indoors for only special events. On February 4, Joel Bailey and his wife went to hear the minstrels.

On Southern plantations, when the master had guests he often called on his slaves to give a show. It would be complete with banjo music and with percussion supplied by a man playing the "bones." Slaves had not been allowed to use drums, because their white masters were afraid they would start riots by signaling each other on the drums as they had done in their native country. But a pair of beef ribs, nicely cleaned and dried, made a satisfying percussion sound.

The minstrel show that the Baileys saw was much different from the original minstrels. There was a Mr. Bones who played the bones, a Mr. Tambo who played the tambourine, and in the center a Mr. Interlocutor who asked questions and made jokes. Most Northern people thought that when they saw a minstrel show, they were "seeing how the Negro slaves had entertained themselves." But they were not. Even the songs they heard had been written especially for the shows and were not really the old Negro songs. But the worst change in the shows since 1870 had been that the portrayal of the Negro characters by white men using black greasepaint actually made fun of the Negro people.

In 1876 a birthday was good for a present and maybe a cake with candles. But the birthday a person celebrated was not necessarily the one that was registered at the city hall or county seat. The doctor, parent, or friend who was going into town, usually sometime after the baby had been born, was asked to stop and register the child's birth. He did not always remember the exact day, and sometimes did not even remember whether it was a boy or a girl. In many cases, the legal records say something like "born about November 10, baby Jones."

George Washington's birthday celebration in 1876 was something special, however. Fervor was starting to build up. Flags flew every place that a flag could be attached—even on baby carriages. It looked like New Year's Eve all over again in every large city in the United States. Carriages and crowds fought for space in the streets. Everywhere there were fireworks—and, consequently, fires.

March and April had their special events too. In New Orleans there was the Mardi Gras. It had been going on now for almost fifty years and getting fancier every time. Colorado was admitted to the union in March, but it would not be official until August 1. April Fools' Day was a great favorite with children who could get away with some pranks for that one day in the year. Some person always fell for the trick of the purse lying on the sidewalk. With visions of reward money he bent down to pick up the purse, when it was suddenly yanked by an unseen string from behind a hedge where kids were howling with laughter.

About four years before, a new holiday had begun in Nebraska. Settlers had cut down the scarce trees to build houses and for burning to keep themselves warm in the winter. A person could ride for miles without seeing a single tree. The publisher of a newspaper in Nebraska City set aside a day for Arbor Day and everyone planted at least one tree. That year a fourteen-year-old boy named Isaac Clagett had planted four thousand slips in only four hours in his Iowa town.

The religious holidays in the spring were very solemn. Even people who never went to church any other Sunday hardly dared stay away on Easter. In 1876 it came on April 16.

The opening day of the Centennial Exhibition was getting nearer. By that time people had to get a pass to get in to see the buildings, but it was worth the effort just to watch some of the unpacking. For weeks ships had been arriving at the port of Philadelphia and each newspaper printed the cargo list. Joel and Susan Bailey had a pass to watch the crates being unpacked one day before the opening. All around them were half-unpacked paintings and statues, some of them, like *The American Volunteer*, astonishing in size. When the Centennial was planned, the American committee members had not been at all prepared for the new type of art coming from Europe. American artists had been painting huge landscape scenes that were so big only the Capitol Building in Washington, D.C., could display them. Americans were used to Grecian statues with plenty of drapery covering them. European sculptors had dispensed with the drapery. Now the works of art were arriving at the Centennial, and the committee had not decided just what to do with them. Workmen had orders not to finish unpacking the nude art yet. Later, those sculptures were banished to the annex and only woodland scenes and battle pictures were in the main Art Museum.

The pieces of art were better treated than the wax exhibit of Cleopatra. She was classified as art, but art was not what most people were thinking about as they crowded into the building to see the figure. She was a life-size figure of flesh-tinted wax reclining on a couch. She even appeared to breathe, her head and eyes moved, and an Ethiopian slave fanned her. A feathery bird fluttered mechanically on the arm of her couch. All this splendor was underneath a golden canopy encased in glass.

"It's a real work of art," said some. "She looks . . . er, alive."

"It's outrageous! Shocking!" said others.

A teen-age boy poses at the feet of the "largest statue of modern times."
The 21½-foot statue of The American Volunteer *was one of the sights of*
the Centennial

Children wait impatiently outside America's first zoo for a glimpse of Rose the grizzly bear or Jennie the elephant

"I guess we'll have to get her out of sight," sighed the art director. Many people never got to see Cleopatra at the Centennial.

While children were waiting for the actual opening day of the Centennial, there was another fascinating place they could visit. America's first zoo had opened just two years before. Adults (25 cents) and children (10 cents) could wander through the zoological gardens and see animals they had only read about before. Children wanted to go first to the bear pits to see "Rose." She was a female grizzly bear and quite a character. Chained by the leg just across from the bear pits was "Jennie," an elephant who seemed to enjoy scaring people. Since her chain could not be seen easily, a timid person would often be startled by Jennie's movements in his direction and he would run for his life. The first zoo also had many strange mammals and birds from Australia—a land that seemed as far away as the moon to most people.

American zookeepers learned within the first two years that different kinds of monkeys have to be kept apart if they are to stay alive. One keeper thought that as long as the prairie dogs were digging holes in their village, the burrowing owls might as well join them. But the owls had to be rescued from the angry prairie dogs.

By 1876, the first zoo could boast that it had most of the animals found in European zoos. There were elephants, giraffes, lions and tigers, zebras, and even "Pete," a rhinoceros bought from P. T. Barnum. The snakes were displayed in the library of a historic home on the zoo property.

At last came May 10, the opening day of the Centennial. With the day came thousands of people. Crowds had been expected, but no one had ever seen such crowds. The celebrated guests, President and Mrs. Ulysses Grant and the Emperor Dom Pedro of Brazil and his wife, were quietly brought in from a side gate or the affair might never have gotten under way.

Decorations were everywhere—on houses, horses, harnesses, baby wagons, baker's wagons, chimneys, lampposts. Everywhere there was red, white, and blue. The motto was well known by now: "1776 with 3 million people on a strip of seacoast; 1876 with 40 million people from ocean to ocean." It was America's proudest moment.

At 9 A.M. the gates opened, and the people began shoving through the turnstiles. The admission fee was a 50-cent note. That did not mean two quarter dollars. Nor did it mean that two people would be admitted for $1. Either a person presented a 50-cent note or he did not get in. It did not work. Angry people shoved quarters and dollars toward the turnstile keepers and leaped over the fences. There never was an accurate total of the number of persons who entered the grounds the first day because the keepers could not get near their foot pedals to register the count.

The rain stopped just in time for the grand opening. As usual for 1876 there were many dull orations, but since there were no microphones, no one could hear the speakers anyway. Most people never did learn the correct name of the Centennial—"The International Exhibition of Arts, Manufactures, and Products of the Soil and Mine." An orchestra of one hundred and fifty pieces, mostly horns and drums, played "Hail Columbia," "The Washington

———·◆◆·———

Rain fell the morning the Centennial opened, but crowds poured through the gates to see President Grant and the Emperor of Brazil

March," and the "Centennial March." There was no national anthem as yet, but the orchestra leader had figured that one of those choices would probably be the anthem some day. Then for forty-five minutes the orchestra played all the national anthems of the other countries taking part in the fair.

President Grant gave a mostly unheard speech and welcomed the Brazilian emperor. At last, a choir of one thousand voices sang the "Hallelujah Chorus" and the Centennial was officially declared open. The Centennial chimes in the tower of Machinery Hall set up a din, a hundred cannons began their salute, and the country's one hundredth birthday party began. The crowds of people had stood as much pomp and pageantry as they could take. They broke through the ropes and ran into the buildings.

The parade of important people fled into the Main Exhibition Building on their way to Machinery Hall, where they were to turn on the giant Corliss engine. Until the Corliss started, no machinery at the fair could work. But the crowds cut off half the party and some people never reached the engine at all. The newspaper excused the crowd later, saying, "The ordinary American was not used to the splendors of uniforms and not often permitted to see ladies in the open air as elegantly dressed as many of them were." A better guess would be that they just wanted to get on with the show.

The two most important men, President Grant and the Emperor, did reach the engine. They got right to business and started the giant engine, and the Exhibition suddenly became alive with noise.

Over at the Ladies' Pavilion, Mrs. Grant was not having so much success. The Empress of Brazil got there first and was asked to open that building officially. By the time Mrs. Grant arrived, there was no special job left for her to do. It was an awkward moment for everyone. The women were especially proud of their building. It had been built with money raised entirely by women and all its exhibits were made by women. It even had its own engine house—with a lady engineer in charge. The women had had to go to Canada to find a lady engineer, but dressed in her trim neat brown dress, she still looked surprisingly like a lady. Her example helped along the ladies' cause for the education of females.

For weeks people had been reading about how large the fair was. But until their aching feet gave out after the first few hours, they had not really believed that there were 80 miles of walks in the grounds. The Main Exhibition Building alone had 11 miles of walks—it was 1,876 feet long. Within a few hours it was clear that no one could hope to see everything in less than two weeks, spending every day at the Exhibition. It was also clear that the fair was not nearly finished yet. Many of the exhibits had not even arrived.

Most of the fair visitors who lived in the city did what Laura Stevens did. She spent one day seeing the Centennial and the next two days getting over it. Then back she went again every third day. On her days off, she filled her journal pages with her impressions: "My first visit to the Great Show. I was too much bewildered to obtain any clear idea out of the Japanese and Chinese departments. It is all immensity, mystery and marvel. . . . Took the rolling chairs for two hours and saw much in a superficial way. . . . The Italian department is full of wonders. . . . I visited the Sandwich Islands [Hawaii now]. . . . We had coffee dispensed after the fashion of Turkey in the Turkish Bazaar. . . . I saw the largest opal in the world ($25,000). . . . A statue of 'Iolanthe' was modeled in butter by a farmer's wife."

The Exposition was open for six months, but all summer people complained because the grounds were not open on Sundays. That was because one of the directors refused to allow anything to break the Sabbath. But the workingmen who had only one day off a week, Sunday, never did get to see the Centennial unless their bosses declared a special holiday.

A narrow-gauge steam railway ran through the park and stopped at all the major buildings. It cost 5 cents a ride, but it traveled 8 miles an hour and many people thought that was too fast. There were ten small engines, each pulling four open cars, constantly carrying tired fair visitors. The rolling chairs, pushed by attendants in gray uniforms, cost 60 cents an hour, or an outrageous $4.50 a day. That price did not look so high after several hours of walking on the asphalt paving that melted like hot lava in the summer sun.

There were exciting moments at the Centennial. A glass keg of wine exploded—fortunately during the night—and sprayed several booths with a smell that outraged many good temperance people. A horse attached to an Adams Express wagon suddenly bolted into the American Restaurant, scattering the customers in all directions. A French restaurant named Three Brothers from Provence charged such high prices ($1.60 for asparagus and $4.60 for roast beef) that a first-day customer complained loudly, "I think each of the three brothers gave me his bill for the meal!"

The Can Can, one of the sideshows filled to overflowing every night, was raided several times. There was no doubt about it—the Can Can was the most shocking event of the year. Mark Twain had seen it first in Paris and his description did nothing to keep the crowds of men away: "I placed my hands before my face for very shame. But I looked through my fingers. . . . A handsome girl . . . grasped her dresses vigorously on both sides with her hands, raised them pretty high, danced an extraordinary jig that had more activity and exposure about it than any jig I ever saw before, and then, drawing her clothes still higher, she advanced gaily to the center and launched a vicious kick."

Americans were very "class" conscious. The Centennial was one of the first occasions where the wealthy actually had to rub elbows with the poor, with country rubes, and even with backwoodsmen wearing leather jackets and moccasins. This was the first time that at least some Americans ever came in contact with "the other half." The Centennial "uniform" seemed to be a brown linen duster for both men and women.

"Foreigners will think it is our national costume," sneered one woman. "There is an utter disregard for the dictates of fashion," complained another. Actually it was just good common sense to dress comfortably. The Centennial was huge beyond anyone's dreams and the summer was sweltering. Fashion designers who had filled the pages of *Godey's Lady's Book* and other fashion books with "dresses to wear to the Centennial" threw up their hands in disgust.

The Centennial had its characters. One fellow from Maine said when he saw the Main Exhibition Building, "I just knowed Maine would beat 'em all!" Then there was the sweet young girl standing with her parasol open over a sundial so that it was completely in shadow—"I never could understand how these things worked, anyway." There was the man from Joplin, Missouri, who had left home in February and pushed his wheelbarrow loaded with Missouri minerals all the way to the fair.

The Centennial police had their hands full with crime of various sorts. One man was arrested and held in $300 bail for prowling around the Centennial at night "in a suspicious manner." He worked ten hours a day, six days a week, and when he was free to see the fair on Sunday, it was not open. Another man, held in $400 bail, had stolen butter and some hot sweet potatoes. A "pocket-picker" was held for $1,000 bail. He was caught with the goods on him—six men's silk pocket handkerchiefs. When not tracking down criminals, the police were busy discouraging such naughty acts as young country couples' holding hands in public.

Sometimes the booth caretakers got bored and had some fun with out-of-town characters. It was not hard to tell which fellows in the homespun clothes had never been to the city before. The newspaper told about a "yokel from Oshkosh" who saw his first oyster. The caretaker told him to go down the next aisle and ask to see the oyster turtle. "We raise oysters on the backs of turtles," he said. Actually, down the next aisle there was a turtle with barnacles on its back, but the country fellow did not know he was being laughed at. The attendant there said, "Well, we don't show that turtle to everyone. But it's not often a real intelligent man asks to see it." Then the poor yokel gets strung along further. "Tell you what," says the attendant. "It's only half after nine o'clock now. Come back about four this afternoon. It's hard to keep enough men to pick the oysters off the turtle's back. If we don't, the weight will drown the turtle. As many as sixty out of a hundred turtles drown here between Saturday and Monday. Take a look every time you're passing here."

Almost every day at the Centennial was a special day. Each state had its day. On Children's Day, the gates opened at 7 A.M. instead of 9 A.M. so that the little people would not get trampled. On Ladies' Day, the prices for men were raised so that the men would stay home. Almost any excuse would do for a special day. But the mayor of Philadelphia received one request that he did not grant. It read: "Dear Sir, We, the So-Called thieves of Philadelphia, are very anxious to see the Centennial and are afraid to go there for fear of Getting Ninety Days we will not Do anything wrong on that Day if you will Be so kind to name a Day for us to Go there you will oblige us very much, Your friends in need."

Most of the Centennial would have to be classified as "educational" for children rather than "fun." The Main Exhibition Building had rows of glass cases displaying various manufactured articles such as cigars, books, corsets, and even silkworm cocoons—"manufactured" by the silkworm. When you saw one, you saw them all. Horticultural Hall was a paradise of flowers, tall palm trees, and tropical plants. Agricultural Hall showed all the newest farming tools, just as Machinery Hall displayed all the latest in engineering technology. But there were some highlights that young people told each other to be sure to look for.

One was the Prismoidal Railway for Rapid Transit. For 5 cents a person could ride across a ravine on a monorail that was shaped like a prism. This was a sample of the rapid transit of the future. The first commercial monorail was even then being built from Norfolk, California, to Sonoma, about three and a half miles away. But the monorail did not catch on that year. Today, one hundred years later, it still may be the rapid transit of the future. The Prismoidal was way ahead of its time.

Another highlight was the Sawyer Observatory. This was not just a simple tower built on a hill. Its round shaft was surrounded by a glass-enclosed circular elevator that climbed 185 feet up to give its passengers a bird's-eye view of the whole Centennial. Only aeronauts who went up in balloons had ever been so high.

About the end of August a new highlight arrived at the Centennial from France. Since it came in several pieces, the main attraction was seeing it put together. The workmen said that it was only a part of a giant statue that was to be built after the Centennial in the harbor of New York City. If that were true, it would be larger than the Colossus of Rhodes, one of the seven wonders of the Ancient World. There was a huge forearm, wrist, and hand. There were several other pieces too that were to be made into a giant

The best bird's-eye view of the Centennial was from Sawyer's observatory—an elevator with windows all around

Few people in 1876 could believe that someday this hand and torch would be a small part of a great statue in New York harbor

torch and flame. The hand alone was so large that six workmen could sit on its wrist while eating their lunch. Putting the many pieces together took great skill and when the workmen had finished, they found an extra thumb left over. They simply put it back into a crate. Soon a stairway was finished inside and visitors could climb up the arm and walk around the base of the torch.

News of the arrival of this part of the statue was not exactly in headlines. In fact, it was listed far down a column of new arrivals, following notice of a deer's antlers stuck in a piece of oak tree. Americans just did not believe that anything as colossal as the Statue of Liberty could be built. Some of the committee had actually laughed at the whole idea when it was first proposed by Edouard de Laboulaye of France. But he was sincere.

"The Statue," he insisted, "is not made of cannon taken on the field of battle. Each of its limbs has not cost a 1,000 men's lives and has not caused countless widows and orphans to shed tears. It will be cast in virgin metal."

The way Monsieur Laboulaye described it, there was really nothing the committee could do but accept "the spirit of the proposal, even if it should prove to be impracticable." Now here was the first portion of the great statue beside a lake at the Centennial. The children climbing up through the arm and walking around the torch could not even begin to understand what they were seeing. Would this really someday be a statue, standing on an island in New York harbor?

There was a playground at the fair, but from the size of it not many children were expected to play there. A merry-go-round with horses and small flatcars to ride on was its main feature. There were also three chair swings and a bench for nursemaids to sit on. Playgrounds were a new idea in 1876, and no one was quite sure how to go about making one.

The Georama attracted quite a bit of attention while it was being built, but not for the right reason. It consisted of small scale models of two cities—Paris and Jerusalem. But it was built outdoors, so when it rained, even a little, the two cities suffered terrible floods, with their houses dramatically floating downstream.

Some of the foreign houses were interesting for children. The

Japanese house was the most popular one of all. A Moorish villa and the Turkish pavilion gave people a chance to glimpse strange parts of the world. Down in the ravine was a Hunters' Camp set up by the Forest and Stream Publishing Company. All the equipment a sportsman could use was on display there, including a "permanent camp" of logs and bark. There were dog kennels, a lake stocked with game fish, game birds, and a trout stream. But it was the camp of a gentleman sportsman and nothing like any camp that Wild Bill Hickok, Buffalo Bill Cody, Wyatt Earp, or even General Custer had ever seen.

Some of the exhibits at the fair made children very hungry. There was a 15-foot-high cathedral of spun white sugar surrounded by historical candy figures, and a 200-pound vase of solid chocolate. Children dragged their parents to the nearest sugar popcorn stand, where they could buy red, white, and blue popcorn balls. Hudnut's soda fountain was the largest in the world and certainly the noisiest, since it had a huge steam calliope. Unfortunately, the calliope player knew only three songs: "Hold the Fort," "In the Sweet Bye and Bye," and "Listen to the Mocking Bird." There was more variety at the soda fountain, where parched throats could be treated with lemonade at 10 cents a glass—there were no paper cups then. Hires Root Beer was brand-new, and so were ice-cream sodas. Every year new flavors were added to the list of iced sodas. Now there was lemon, sarsaparilla, ginger ale and birch beer. On a hot day, Hudnut's sold 3,500 glassfuls. Peanuts could be bought outside the Centennial grounds, but the committee had voted not to allow them to be brought inside because the shells made too much litter for the "broom brigade" to clean up every night. For children without any money, there was always the Catholic Total Abstinence Fountain where water poured constantly over large blocks of ice.

"Old Abe," the War Eagle of Wisconsin, was high on the list of "must see's" for the children. His background history was impressive, but not necessarily true. Supposedly he had been taken from his nest by an Indian, Chief Sky, and sold to a soldier from Wisconsin for a bushel of corn. His war record was true, however. Old Abe had become the mascot and served three years with the 8th regiment from Wisconsin during the War Between the States.

One Southern general is supposed to have said, "I would rather capture Old Abe than a whole brigade."

One exhibit attracted children like flies, yet they could hardly stand to look at it. It was the one presented by the Society for the Prevention of Cruelty to Animals. Henry Bergh of New York had been fighting for animals for a long time. When he saw live turtles in the market with their flippers tied cruelly together, he was angry. When he saw live pigeons being shot for sport, he was furious and suggested that the sportsmen use "clay pigeons." Mr. Bergh was not perfect. He also was annoyed at P. T. Barnum for not giving his rhinoceros a tub of water to bathe in, until he was told that rhinos were not like hippos and did not care for water. But Mr. Bergh did not have to go very far to see animals being used cruelly all around him. His booth at the Centennial was full of grisly proof that animals were really suffering at the hands of humans.

He had on display gamecocks that had been stuffed *after* the fights that had killed them. People made bets on which cock would win, and the fight was not over until one was dead. The same was done with dogs, and the S.P.C.A. exhibit had some stuffed dogs to show their wounds. Among other trophies was the leg bone of a horse that had been forced to walk with a broken leg. There were collections of whips, each with the name of the owner who had used it to beat an animal. A simple red brick had a note telling its story—it had been thrown at a horse by an angry driver and had broken two of the horse's ribs. The driver, August Sann, had been fined $25 and had spent a month in the penitentiary.

On a boy's list one of the sights to see was the Krupp cannon. It was no longer the largest in the world, but a story connected with it increased its value. A war was going on in Constantinople and when the cannon was halfway to the United States for the Centennial Exhibition, its makers had sold it to the Turkish government. However, it was still to be shown at the fair. The war would just have to wait.

One of the most important exhibits at the fair was probably seen by very few children. It is called the telephone today, but at that time not even its inventor, Alexander Graham Bell, had decided what to call it. Not many people were excited about his invention, but scientists were. A few of them wanted the Emperor of Brazil to be sure to hear it work while he was at the Centennial. But there was so much noise he could not hear. One of the scientists suggested coming back on a Sunday when there was no one else around. "It works!" the Emperor gasped with surprise.

Most children wanted to see "Shantyville" as well as the Centennial, but they had a hard time talking their parents into it. Shantyville was also called "Dinkeytown" and the "Honky-tonk Midway." It was the area that lined the street on the way to the main entrance. Shantyville did not close at night. In fact, it did its best business when the Centennial had been put to bed.

From all sides, barkers called out to passersby to tempt them with delights on their way into the fairgrounds. There were the "man-eating Feejees," the "wild men of Borneo," and the Wild Children from Australia. Every day a chair was broken by a 602-pound fat lady. Who wanted to miss seeing the two-legged horse, the five-legged cow, or the educated pig that could do tricks? In the ugly unpainted wooden stalls, lunch could be bought much cheaper than inside the gates. Children could choose their "vittles" from such delectables as caramels, peanuts, hot-roasted potatoes, oranges, and lemonade. There were pie stalls, men and women selling polished apples, Bologna sausage, cakes, and balloons. Children could not understand why their parents always hustled them past Shantyville and places like the Can Can Palace.

Before the Centennial was over, Shantyville caught fire and burned down one September afternoon. "At last! The bonfire we expected," the newspaper reported without much sympathy. In two hours, the four acres of Shantyville were a smoking waste. Gone forever was Murphy's oyster saloon, Kretzer's ice cream and oyster saloon, several beer saloons, a variety show house, and the strange animals. The educated pig escaped. Even the shooting gallery, the Oriental saloon, and several cheap boardinghouses were gone. Mr. Léotard, the gymnast, had to escape in his tights, which probably made him famous, because tights have been called "leotards" ever since. The girls at the Jardin Mabille ran outside in their petticoats. Such a huge crowd gathered to watch the excitement that the firemen could not fight the fire. The buildings that did not burn down were ordered torn down by the mayor, who had not approved of Shantyville from the start.

During the summer, people began to get sick. "Centennial fever" was what out-of-town newspapers called it. They warned people not to drink any water at the Centennial. "Allay your thirst," they advised, "by chewing bits of leather or even shingle nails. Get plenty of rest and don't breathe within the city limits." The Philadelphia newspapers said that the sickness was from overeating and sitting on the doorsteps on a hot summer evening. Doctors said it looked very much like typhoid fever. The fair was as large as a whole new city, and its drainage system was not good enough to take care of all the extra sewage.

Americans were surprised to learn that the most wonderful inventions at the Centennial had all been discovered during the previous ten years. Here was proof that they were living right in the middle of a wonderful age. Hundreds of lasting changes came about just because of the Centennial. A medical exhibit from Belgium took away people's fear of the smallpox vaccine. Joseph Lister spoke to a group of medical men about his "germ theory," and within a few years people would finally understand what caused diseases and would begin to work on ways to prevent them. All the countries taking part in the Exhibition compared notes on many of the problems they shared. One country had a superior way of teaching the blind to read. Another had a better way to make false teeth so they would fit. Women compared needlework samples, foods, and styles of clothing.

The Centennial began on the tenth of May, but it was crowded every single day until it closed in November. In other parts of the country, people who could not go to the Centennial still had their special events.

The children of Newton, Iowa, were all excited on the twentieth of May. The W. W. Coles Roman Racing Hippodrome was coming. Almost the whole town was waiting at the railroad station when the special circus train pulled in. Dozens of boys volunteered their muscles for unloading and setting up the monstrous tent. A preview of the night's attractions was given as the circus performers and animals paraded through the main street.

That night, Iowans paid 50 cents each—25 cents for children under ten—to see a "Brand New Show on a Stupendous Scale . . . All Former Attempts in Show Business were Completely Eclipsed." There was enough canvas, poles, tackle, rope, chains, and masts to outfit a fleet of ships. Inside the tent, a "Monster" racetrack 30 feet wide was built. Charioteers raced blindfolded and even backward. The townspeople took part in a "walking match." There were clown-and-donkey races where the slowest won, followed by "Wild Horses" to be turned loose on the track. Elephants, camels, dromedaries, Spanish bulls, bison, reindeer, zebras—every sort of animal that could be kept alive on such a trip was lined up for the "Zoological Garden Promenade."

At 10 P.M. a cannon was fired to announce the Mardi-Gras Pageant through the streets. Three bands, including a mechanical steam calliope that could be heard ten miles away, guaranteed that no one would sleep through the big event.

Decoration Day had begun in the South where the women always decorated the graves of their soldiers with flowers at the end of May. Soon they were doing the same for the graves of the Northern soldiers too. In 1868, General John Logan proclaimed a special day to honor the graves of all soldiers. By 1876, it was the custom for everyone to visit the graves of his loved ones and leave flowers. President Lincoln's grave in Springfield, Illinois, was always decorated with sprays of pine from the North and palmetto from the South.

Julia Ward Howe was one of the important feminists in 1876, but she was remembered best for her poem "The Battle Hymn of the Republic." She was trying to talk Americans into setting aside one day in June to be called Mother's Day. It was not official, but mothers in Boston were already enjoying a special day.

The Fourth of July had been the nation's most important special day for a hundred years. But in 1876 that date raised a record whooping and hollering. Since it fell on a Tuesday, many businesses closed so their people could begin celebrating on Saturday—taking off Sunday for a day of rest, of course. Every city had something special scheduled. San Francisco had a sham battle in the harbor, followed by a carnival ball. Boston had balloon ascensions and regattas all day. New York City had parades.

Even Deadwood, in the Dakota Territory, was not quiet. A disaster had just happened nearby, but most folks refused to believe it. This was the weekend of the "cowboy tournament," and Deadwood was ready for the thousands of cowhands that would be in town to celebrate the end of a long cattle drive. The mining men and gamblers arranged for a roping contest with $200 for prize money.

"We picked the wildest mustangs this year any cowboy ever saw," said the men. Each group of cowboys picked its champion to compete. Six were Negroes who had ridden the range all their lives. Winner of the roping contest, though, was Nat Love, known as "Red River Dick." He landed a mustang only nine minutes from the crack of the gun.

After the roping contest, the men started arguing about who was the best shot. In the afternoon, a shooting contest was held. Each contestant had fourteen shots with a rifle and twelve with a Colt. Nat Love won that contest, too, and from then on was called "Deadwood Dick."

The wildest Fourth of July celebration that year was probably in Philadelphia, where thousands were already gathered to see the Centennial. Two hundred thousand visitors stormed through the railroad station in one day. "The depot is filled with valises [suitcases] and many will have no change of clothes for tomorrow," a newspaper wailed.

Twenty thousand men paraded through the city carrying torches. Hotels had people sleeping on people. The parade that was to go down Chestnut Street to Independence Hall never made it, because the spectators would not stay off the street. Scattered in with the crowd were terrified, rearing horses. On all sides fireworks and cap pistols (new in 1876) were exploding. All the restaurants were out of food before dinner time. There was not a crust of bread left in town by evening. Fireworks had started several fires. Steam fire engines were trying vainly to reach the blazes.

Amid all this uproar, there were still the inevitable orations going on at Independence Hall. People close enough to hear the chorus and orchestra were surprised at the song chosen for this occasion. It was "The Star-spangled Banner"—a song everyone said could be sung only by opera stars.

Richard Henry Lee of Virginia read the original manuscript of the Declaration of Independence to the 150,000 people in front of Independence Hall. Right after Lee, a poet named Bayard Taylor was to recite his "National Ode." But as Taylor stood on one side of the platform reading his "Ode," there was a commotion at the other side.

Susan B. Anthony and four of her staunchest supporters stamped up onto the platform. While Mrs. Anthony read her revised "Declaration of Independence for Women," her helpers passed out copies of what she was reading so that no one could say he did not hear. The other people on the platform were so surprised that they did nothing to stop her. In a well-trained voice that easily outshouted the poet, Mrs. Anthony read her document to the audience. As she finished, the women marched out again, singing their theme song. They had made their point.

The sensational excitement of July 4 died down fast when the telegraph ticked away its unhappy message the next day. A steamboat had come with news from Dakota Territory about the Battle of the Little Big Horn. General Custer and his gallant 7th Cavalry troops were dead. The newspapers thought up a new motto: "John Bull 1776—Sitting Bull 1876." It was not exactly true that Sitting Bull had been responsible this time, but the motto was catchy, so Sitting Bull took the blame for the tragedy.

What had gone wrong? Probably the whole story will never be known. Custer had seen shipments of new Springfield rifles being sent up the river to trading posts and he knew that the Indians were buying them. They were far better guns than his own men had. When word came that he would have to face the Indians, he was concerned about those guns. But his reliable scouts had assured him that there were only about twelve hundred Indians.

Later, after Custer had left with his men, other scouts discovered new Indian trails leading down from the country north of the Big Horn Mountains. One was a half mile wide. There were at least five thousand Indians waiting for the 7th Cavalry! Some scouts rode off to warn the general, but it was too late. Isaiah Dorman, a black scout, was one of those to reach Custer just in time to join the battle.

The uprising was the beginning of the end for the Indians. There had been prejudice before the battle, but after it few whites would help them with their growing problems. They were packed into reservations as fast as possible. Even Indians who had never caused trouble were treated with hatred.

On August 1, Colorado officially became the thirty-eighth state. Artists began thinking how to arrange the stars on the flag, because a new flag had to be ready by the next July 4. One idea was to have 5 rows of stars, alternating between 8 stars in one row and 7 in the next. Or 6 rows of stars, with 7 stars in the 1st and 6th rows and only 6 stars in the other rows. The prettiest design had the stars arranged to spell out 1776 and 1876. But even though Colorado caused a flag problem, it was a welcome addition. Gold had been discovered there and in the past year rich veins of silver and lead ore were also found. But the Rocky Mountains in Colorado, which are so appreciated by Americans today, were considered a serious drawback in 1876.

November 7 was Election Day. There were no computers to count the votes quickly, and for several months both sides thought they had won. Congress finally had to set up an electoral commission (now called a college) the next January to try to decide who was to be the next president. Samuel J. Tilden thought he was, because he had 184 electoral votes. But he needed 185 to get a majority. Rutherford B. Hayes, the Republican candidate, was not far behind—he had 165. Twenty votes were in doubt. The electoral commission tried hard to be fair, but the Republicans on it outnumbered the Democrats and they gave the 20 votes to Hayes. The decision came just in time so that he could be sworn into office in March 1877.

For over fifteen years, Sarah Josepha Hale, the editor of *Godey's Lady's Book*, had been trying to talk American families into setting aside a Thursday late in November as a day of thanksgiving. By 1863 she had even convinced President Lincoln that the last Thursday in November should be Thanksgiving Day. Only in recent years has it been changed by presidential order to come earlier in the month to extend the Christmas season.

Imagine Christmas without Santa Claus parades or department stores filled with overflowing shelves and customers! In 1876 there were no special lights outside stores or down streets. A few of the larger stores had "a Christmas window," usually filled with toys that were to be handed out to orphans on Christmas Eve.

Christmas trees were still a fairly new idea in America. People did not buy a tree. They chopped their own and carried it home on a sled. The tree was decorated with strings of popcorn and cranberries. People who could afford to bought delicate glass ornaments imported from Germany, but most people had to be satisfied with ornaments they made themselves. The only lights on the tree were tiny candles. While the tree was still freshly cut and sitting in water to keep it from dying too fast, the candles were fairly safe. But as soon as the tree began to dry out, the flame from the candles was deadly. Many people were killed every year when their Christmas trees caught fire.

Only rich children were taken to toy stores. Poor children gaped through the window at the wonders inside

One of the first "Christmas windows" in New York. The dolls in the scene were given away to orphans Christmas Eve, 1876

Santa Claus was no "right jolly old elf" in 1876. Only the year before, a book had shown the first picture of Santa that even made him look pleasant. He was short and fat, wore a turban for a cap, and his coat was trimmed with white fur. Until then, Saint Nicholas had looked as if he did not even have a sense of humor. Children hung their stockings "by the chimney with care," but almost every stocking had at least one little piece of coal in it along with the other small surprises on Christmas morning to remind them that, although they had been good enough to get presents from Santa, they had not been perfect all year. Almost every stocking had an orange in the toe. A real orange in the middle of winter was a treat that could not be found in just any neighborhood grocery store.

"Going caroling" was a favorite excuse for young people to get together in the wintertime. Rehearsals were held—probably for more evenings than necessary. Then the group went out caroling on

Christmas Eve. It was another way for boys and girls to get acquainted with each other.

Not many people bought Christmas presents in stores. Those toys were too expensive for most fathers' paychecks. There were lovely dolls from France whose dresses were as intricate as real ladies' dresses. Sturdy iron fire engines and horse-drawn trolleys and stagecoaches made little boys happy. One toy loved by a boy was a house on fire. The house stood about two feet tall. On the roof and on the balcony were two ladies calling for help. The firemen climbed the ladders when the toy was wound up and working. Every boy wanted a cap pistol. Some were just like guns, but others had gadgets that worked when the trigger was pulled. There was a marble shooter too that "picks up and discharges marbles with rifle-like accuracy" and sounds dangerous. There were no rules about safe toys that could not blind or hurt children. A new Buffalo Bill revolver with one hundred cartridges cost $3. A big present was a "magic lantern" with slides. But few people could afford the $100 for one.

Most presents for Christmas were handmade. For many weeks before the holiday every member in the family found himself a secret hiding place for the presents he was making. A children's magazine gave one hundred suggestions of things to make.

A girl of six or seven could make a "scent case" for her mother or sister to keep handkerchiefs in. Or she might make a washstand frill—that was a ruffle to be nailed above the washstand so the wall would not get splashed. For older girls, who could sew better, there were suggestions such as a sandbag case for grandmother. That was just what it sounds like—a case for a bag full of sand. When grandmother went to church or went out in the carriage in the winter, the bag of sand was first warmed up in the oven and then for at least two hours, it would keep grandmother's feet warm.

Daughter might sew some square flat cases for Papa so he could keep his removable shirt cuffs clean. Penwipers were a usual present for Papa from the little members of the family who could not sew well. Fountain pens had not been invented yet, and Papa was always needing something to wipe his pen, because homemade ink gummed up the point as it dried. "Cabin bags" were a perfect gift for someone going on a trip. They had rows of little pockets to hold all the small things that got "lost in the tumble and toss of a voyage." Another gift for travelers was tiny satin cases filled with pleasant-smelling herbs. Clothes that were packed for a week inside a trunk smelled like leather for weeks afterward unless scent bags (sachets) were tucked into all the folds of the clothing.

What did a young girl receive for Christmas in 1876? Mary Elizabeth Jonas got a sealskin purse, gold sleeve buttons to sew on her best dress, a workbasket, a lace handkerchief for parties, a blue pincushion, and a book of poems. She gave her best boyfriend a picture of "Dante's Inferno."

New Year's Eve of 1876 was not nearly so exciting as the night that had started off the year. The great Centennial year was over and such special days might never be seen again. But, as everyone knows now, very special days were really on the way.

BIBLIOGRAPHY

Here are some of the books that helped provide the background for what life was like in 1876.

The American Heritage Book of the Pioneer Spirit. By the Editors of *American Heritage,* American Heritage Publishing Co., Inc., distributed by Simon & Schuster, Inc., 1959.

Bolton, Henry C., *Counting-Out Rhymes of Children: A Study in Folklore.* London, 1888.

Botkin, B. A. (ed.), *A Treasury of American Folklore.* Crown Publishers, 1944.

Brown, Dee, *The Year of the Century: 1876.* Charles Scribner's Sons, 1966.

Brubacher, John S., *A History of Problems of Education.* McGraw-Hill Book Co., Inc., 1947.

Burchell, S. C., *Age of Progress.* Time-Life Books, 1966.

Carruth, Gorton, & Associates (eds.), *Encyclopedia of American Facts and Dates.* 6th ed. The Thomas Y. Crowell Company, 1972.

Carson, Gerald, *The Old Country Store.* E. P. Dutton & Co., Inc., 1965.

—— *One for a Man; Two for a Horse.* Doubleday & Company, Inc., 1961.

Chapelle, H. I., *History of American Sailing Ships.* Bonanza Books, 1935.

Chase, Gilbert, *America's Music.* Rev. 2d ed. McGraw-Hill Book Co., Inc., 1966.

Crampton, C. Gregory, *Land of Living Rock.* Alfred A. Knopf, Inc., 1972.

Cubberley, Elwood, *The History of Education.* Houghton Mifflin Company, 1948.

Custer, Elizabeth B., *Boots and Saddles*. Harper & Brothers, 1885.

Davidson, Marshall B., *The American Heritage History of Notable American Houses*. American Heritage Publishing Co., Inc., 1971.

Devens, R. M., *Our First Century*. C. A. Nichols & Company, 1880.

Dunaway, Philip, and Evans, Mel (eds.), *A Treasury of the World's Great Diaries*. Doubleday & Company, Inc., 1957.

Durham, Philip, and Jones, Everett L., *The Negro Cowboys*. Dodd, Mead & Company, Inc., 1965.

Furnas, J. C., *Goodbye to Uncle Tom*. William Sloane Associates, Inc., 1956.

Gibbons, Euell, *Stalking the Good Life*. David McKay Company, Inc., 1971.

Godwin, John, *This Baffling World*. Hart Publishing Co., Inc., 1968.

Gondos, Dorothy, *The Cultural Climate of Centennial City, Philadelphia*. Ph.D. thesis on microfilm, 1947.

Green, John R., M.D., *Medical History for Students*. Charles C Thomas, Publisher, 1968.

Groner, Alex, with the Editors of *American Heritage* and *Business Week* magazines, *The History of American Business and Industry*. American Heritage Publishing Co., Inc., 1972.

Hale, William Harlan, *The Horizon Cookbook*. American Heritage Publishing Co., Inc., 1968.

Hall, Carrie, *Review of the Follies and Foibles of Fashion, 1866–1936: From Hoopskirts to Nudity*. Caxton Printers, Ltd., 1938.

Holt, Rackham, *George Washington Carver*. Doubleday & Company, Inc., 1943.

Idell, Albert E., *Centennial Summer*. Henry Holt & Company, Inc., 1943.

Konikow, Robert B., *Discover Historic America*. Rand McNally & Company, 1973.

Kouwenhoven, John A., *Adventures of America, 1857–1900*. Harper & Brothers, 1938.

The Life Treasury of American Folklore. By the Editors of Life and Time, Inc., 1961.

McCabe, James D., *Our Young Folks Abroad*. J. B. Lippincott Company, 1887.

Manual of the Graded Course of Instruction. Burk & McFetridge, Printers, 1884.

Marks, Geoffrey, and Beatty, William K., *Women in White*. Charles Scribner's Sons, 1972.

Mattfeld, Julius, *Variety Music Cavalcade*. Prentice-Hall, Inc., 1971.

Meltzer, Milton, producer, *Mark Twain Himself: A Pictorial Biography.* Bonanza Books, 1960.

Menke, Frank G., *The Encyclopedia of Sports.* 4th rev. ed. A. S. Barnes & Company, Inc., 1969.

Morgan, George, *Philadelphia: The City of Firsts.* Historical Publications Society of Philadelphia, 1926.

Morris, John V., *Fires and Firefighters.* Little, Brown & Company, 1955.

Payne, Blanche, *History of Costume.* Harper & Row, Publishers, Inc., 1965.

Pike, James, *The Philadelphia Shipping Manual, 1876.*

Randel, William Peirce, *Centennial: American Life in 1876.* Chilton Book Company, 1969.

Ruth, John A., *Decorum: A Practical Treatise on Etiquette and Dress of the Best American Society.* J. A. Ruth Company, 1879.

Schmitt, Martin F., and Brown, Dee, *The Settlers' West.* Charles Scribner's Sons, 1955.

Shryock, Richard Harrison, *Medicine in America: Historical Essays.* The Johns Hopkins Press, 1966.

Sprague, Marshall, *A Gallery of Dudes.* Little, Brown & Company, 1967.

Stimpson, George, *A Book About a Thousand Things.* Harper's, 1946.

Taylor, Frank H., and Schoff, Wilfred H., *The Port and City of Philadelphia.* Local organizing commission of the 12th International Congress of Navigation, Philadelphia, 1912.

Trout, S. Edgar, *The Story of the Centennial of 1876, Golden Anniversary.* Copyright 1929, S. E. Trout.

Tyree, Marion Cabell, *Housekeeping in Old Virginia.* John P. Morton & Company, 1879.

Van Deusen, John G., *The Black Man in White America.* Rev. ed. Associated Publishers, Inc., 1944.

Walker, Francis A. (ed.), *Reports and Awards, International Exhibition, 1876.* J. B. Lippincott Company, 1878.

Wallace, Irving, *The Fabulous Show Man.* Alfred A. Knopf, Inc., 1959.

Washington, Booker T., *Up from Slavery: An Autobiography.* Dodd, Mead & Company, Inc., 1965.

Whiting, Emma Mayhew, and Hough, Henry Beetle, *Whaling Wives.* Houghton Mifflin Company, 1953.

Wigginton, Eliot (ed.), *The Foxfire Book.* Doubleday & Company, Inc., 1972.

Wilcox, R. Turner, *The Dictionary of Costume.* Charles Scribner's Sons, 1969.

——— *Five Centuries of American Costume.* Charles Scribner's Sons, 1963.

Williams, T. Harry, and the Editors of *Life, The Union Restored.* Life History of U.S., Vol. 6, 1861–1876. Time-Life Books, 1963.

Wilson, Charles Morrow, *Ambassadors in White.* Henry Holt & Company, Inc., 1942.

Wilson, Harold F., *The Story of the Jersey Shore.* D. Van Nostrand Company, Inc., 1964.

The World Book Encyclopedia. Field Enterprises Educational Corporation, 1958.

Young, James Harvey, *The Toadstool Millionaires.* Princeton University Press, 1961.

But just setting the background was not enough. It was essential to read some of the same books and magazines and newspapers that people had in their homes during the year 1876. Here are some of them.

Appleton's Annual Cyclopaedia and Register of Important Events of the Year 1876. New Series, Vol. I. D. Appleton & Company, 1877.

Appleton's Journal of Literature, Science and Art, 1875. Magazines.

Bartlett, John Russell, *Dictionary of Americanism.* A Glossary of Words and Phrases usually regarded as peculiar to the U.S. Bartlett & Wilford, 1848.

Beeton, Mrs. Isabella, *The Book of Household Management.* London: S. O. Beeton, 1861. Published in the United States by Farrar, Straus & Giroux, Inc., 1969.

Brooks, Edward, *The New Normal Mental Arithmetic.* Sower, Potts & Company, 1873.

Busch, William, *Max and Moritz, A Juvenile History in Seven Tricks.* Roberts Brothers, 1876.

Chavasse, Pye Henry, *Advice to a Wife and Mother.* George Routledge & Sons, 1873.

Churchill, Fleetwood, M.D., *On the Diseases of Infants and Children.* Lea and Blanchard, 1850.

Circulars of Information of the Bureau of Education, No. 1, 1875. Government Printing Office, 1875.

Coffin, C. A., *Centennial City Philadelphia, A Complete Guide for Strangers, 1876.*

Cornell, S. S., *Cornell's Intermediate Geography*. D. Appleton & Company, 1855.

Cousin Virginia, The Christmas Stocking. Thomas O'Kane Publishers, 1875.

Dio, Lewis, M.D., *Our Girls*. Harper & Brothers Publishers, 1871.

Eclectic Magazine of Foreign Literature, Science and Art, 1876 issues.

Epes, Sargent, and May, Amasa, *The New American First Reader*. E. H. Butler & Company, 1871.

Frank Leslie's Illustrated Almanac for 1876.

Frank Leslie's Illustrated Newspapers, 1876 issues.

Godey's Lady's Book, 1876 issues.

Gopsill, James, *Philadelphia City Directory, 1875*. Published by James Gopsill, Philadelphia, Pa., 1875.

Harper's Weekly, 1876 issues.

The Illustrated Manners Book: A Manual of Good Behavior and Polite Accomplishments. Leland Clay & Company, 1855.

Important Events of the Century. U.S. Central Publishing Company, 1876.

The Independent. Boston and New York newspaper, 1876 issues.

Ingram, John S., *The Centennial Exhibition, Described and Illustrated*. Hubbard, 1876.

The Jenkintown Pestle. Small Pennsylvania newspaper, 1875 issues.

Journal of the Society of Arts, Vol. XXIV, Nov. 19, 1875, to Nov. 10, 1876. Published for the Society by George Bell & Sons, London, 1876.

Lippincott's Magazine, 1876 issues.

Loring, Laurie, *The Holiday Album for Girls*. D. Lothrop & Company, 1875.

McCabe, James D., *Illustrated History of the Centennial Exhibition*. National Publishing Company, 1876.

Mackarness, Mrs. Henry, *The Young Lady's Book: A Manual of Amusements, Exercises, Studies and Pursuits*. George Routledge & Sons, 1876.

Monroe's Fifth Reader, 1871.

Newspapers from every city in the United States, dated May, 1876. Kept in the Archives of the City of Philadelphia.

Norton, Frank B., *The Illustrated Historical Register of the U.S. Centennial Exhibition*. Subscription Book Department, The American News Company, 1876.

Official Catalogue of the U.S. International Exhibition, 1876. Rev. ed. John R. Nagle and Company, Riverside Press, 1876.

Old and New, January–May 1875. Library of Congress, Washington, 1875.

Oliver Optic's Magazine, 1874 issues. Lee & Shepard, 1874.

Optic, Oliver, or Adams, W. T., *Going West, or The Perils of a Poor Boy*. Lee & Shepard, 1875.

Our Young Folks. Illustrated magazine for boys and girls, 1873 issues.

Peterson's Magazine, 1876 issues.

Philadelphia Public Ledger. Newspaper, 1876 issues.

Raymond, R. W., *The Man in the Moon and Other People*. The American News Company, 1876.

Report of the 27th Exhibition of American Manufactures. Held in the City of Philadelphia, October 6 to November 12, 1874, by the Franklin Institute, William P. Kildare, Printer, Philadelphia, 1874.

Scribner's Monthly Magazine, 1876 issues.

Spencer, Herbert, *Education: Intellectual, Moral, and Physical*. D. Appleton & Company, 1860 (reprinted 1917).

St. Nicholas Magazine. November 1875 to October 1876 issues. Scribner's Illustrated Magazine for Girls and Boys, Scribner & Company.

Strahan, Edward, *A Century After: Picturesque Glimpses of Philadelphia and Pennsylvania*. Allen, Lane & Scott, 1875.

Tanner, Thomas Hawkes, M.D., *The Practice of Medicine*. Lindsay & Blakiston, 1866.

Timbs, John, *Notabilia or Curious and Amusing Facts About Many Things*. London: Griffith & Farran, 1872.

Webster, Noah, *An American Dictionary of the English Language*. George and Charles Merriam, 1860.

Westcott, Thompson, *The Official Guide Book to Philadelphia*. Porter & Coates, 1875.

The Woman's Journal. Magazine edited by Julia Ward Howe, Boston, 1876.

The rest of the information for this book on the year 1876 came from the diaries and journals of the individuals who actually lived then. A few of the diaries had been published in books already listed. But many more were found at the Historical Society of Pennsylvania, at Mystic Seaport Library, and in someone's attic. These persons were the real eyewitnesses to the way it was—in 1876.

INDEX

Italicized numbers indicate illustrations